Herbert Vaughan

Submission to a divine teacher neither disloyalty nor the surrender of mental and moral freedom

A pastoral letter

Herbert Vaughan

Submission to a divine teacher neither disloyalty nor the surrender of mental and moral freedom
A pastoral letter

ISBN/EAN: 9783337282745

Printed in Europe, USA, Canada, Australia, Japan

Cover: Foto ©Lupo / pixelio.de

More available books at **www.hansebooks.com**

Rt. Rev. Herbert Vaughan, D.D., on Mr. Gladstone.

SUBMISSION TO A DIVINE TEACHER

NEITHER DISLOYALTY

NOR THE SURRENDER OF

MENTAL AND MORAL FREEDOM.

A PASTORAL LETTER.

BY

HERBERT, BISHOP OF SALFORD.

NEW YORK:
THE CATHOLIC PUBLICATION SOCIETY,
No. 9 WARREN STREET.

NOTE.

I avail myself of the call for another issue of this Pastoral, to add a few notes and some appendices in further elucidation of what has been already said. The appendices chiefly regard three points: (1) The right and occasionally the duty of the clergy to take part in certain political questions; (2) The answer given by Dr. von Döllinger to those who, as he says, "especially in Germany and England, brand the Papal power as being boundless, as being absolutist, as one which recognizes no law capable of controlling it." This answer must derive a special value, not only from the fact that it is directed to Englishmen, but from its occurring in one of the last works published by the Professor. We must regard it as the mature and deliberate judgment of an author who had been thirty-five years before the world, and whose whole life had been engaged in the study of Church and Papal history. It may be supposed that Mr. Gladstone will be ready to admit that we shall find in Professor v. Döllinger, if anywhere, what he calls "the truth and authority of history and the inestimable value of the historic spirit" (p. 14).

Lastly (3), there is the subject of Mariolatry." Mr. Gladstone has characterized the Definition of the Immaculate Conception as "a violent breach with history," a "deadly blow," "an act of violence," a hurrying on, and a precipitating of a doctrine of "Mariolatry." To enter upon this subject at any length would be to exceed my limits. But I will call attention to a work just issued from the press, entitled "Our Lady's Dowry," by the Rev. T. E. Bridgett, C.SS.R. (Burns & Oates). It is not a work of controversy, but of historical research into the belief, love, and practices of Englishmen over a thousand years ago down to the sixteenth century, in regard to our Blessed Lady. Though not intended as such, it is an unanswerable refutation of Mr. Gladstone's charge of "a violent breach with history." Indeed, the tables are completely reversed. I shows how England obtained in Europe the title of "Our Lady's Dowry," and how she lost it. Calmly and historically it proves that they are not Catholics, but Mr. Gladstone and others who have made "a violent breach with history" by their rejection of the love and worship of our Blessed Lady. It will be seen that "the deadly blows" were aimed not "in 1854 and 1870," but in 1536 and 1559, not by Catholics but by Protestants, "at the old historic, scientific, and moderate school." But, despite "deadly blows" and "acts of violence," the old historic and scientific thread of devotion to Our Lady and belief in her Immaculate Conception have been preserved to England—preserved by the very "school" which is now once more assailed for that religious constancy and love for Mary, in which, by God's grace, it will never fail.

In my judgment, "Our Lady's Dowry" is the most excellent, the most interesting, and the most original work of its kind and for its purpose that has been published in the English language. I strongly recommend it to the Clergy and to all educated Englishmen, whether Catholic or non-Catholic, who have any care to investigate the religious history of their country.

✜ HERBERT, Bishop of Salford.

January 1, 1875.

CONTENTS.

		PAGE.
I.—THE ACCUSATION,		7
II.—OUR GENERAL PRINCIPLES ON ALLEGIANCE,		8
(1.) Meaning and Duty of Civil and Spiritual Allegiance,		8
(2.) In what is the Spiritual Power invested?		13
III.—A DIVINE TEACHER CLAIMS THE REASONABLE SUBMISSION OF OUR MENTAL AND MORAL NATURE,		15
(1.) Clear from Reason,		15
IV.—OUR DIVINE LORD'S PRINCIPLE AND PLAN OF TEACHING,		17
(1.) Authority and Obedience approved to Reason,		17
V.—HIS CHURCH FOUNDED AS A DIVINE TEACHER ON THE SAME PRINCIPLE AND PLAN,		20
(1.) Divine because of its Constitution,		20
(2.) " " of its Divine Principle,		21
(3.) " " of its Divine Headship,		23
(4.) " " of its Divine Animating "Spirit,"		25
VI.—THE ROMAN CATHOLIC AND APOSTOLIC CHURCH THE DIVINE TEACHER,		27
(1.) Her Marks, Dogmatic and Historical,		27
VII.—INFALLIBILITY OF THE DIVINE TEACHER,		30
(1.) Infallibility: When and Why Defined,		30
(2.) The Vatican Decree,		32
(3.) Its Restriction,		33
(4.) What it is that the World hates,		34
(5.) The Döllingerites,		35

		PAGE
VIII.—SOME COUNTS OF ACCUSATION,		36
(1.) Mental Slavery of Catholics,		36
(2.) Scandals—Lord Acton,		39
(3.) Church and State in Conflict,		41
(4.) Papal Infallibility, a *new* danger,		43
(5.) Catholic loyalty questioned—a trap,		48
(6.) "But the deposing Power"!		51
(7.) Catholic Freedom in matters political,		53
(8.) Practising on "the open and trustful temper,"		54
(9.) Indictment of the Syllabus,		57
IX.—CONCLUSION,		59

APPENDICES—

    A. Dr. v. Döllinger on the growth, office, power, limitations, and perpetuity of the Papacy, ... 61

    B. Innocent III.'s limitation of the Papal Power, ... 71

    C. Curious statistical contrast arising out of "The rights of man" and the Deposing Power, ... 72

    D. The interference of the Clergy in certain political questions, ... 72

    E. The Immaculate Conception, historically, . 75

HERBERT, by the Grace of God and of the Apostolic See, Bishop of Salford, to the Clergy, Secular and Regular, and to the Faithful of the said Diocese,

HEALTH AND BENEDICTION IN THE LORD.

DEARLY BELOVED BRETHREN AND CHILDREN IN JESUS CHRIST,—

We speak to you once more, as the Father and Pastor who will have to render an account to God for your souls, so "that the trial of your faith (much more precious than gold which is tried by the fire,) may be found unto praise and glory and honour." (1 *Peter* i.7.)

A topic affecting your honour and your religion is in the minds of all. It is due to you that we should speak, and lay down for your guidance certain general principles upon which you can neither be shaken nor led astray.

I.—THE ACCUSATION.

The brief statement of the case is this:—

In an evil hour, an illustrious politician, whose distinguished services to justice we shall not forget, has descended from the noble eminence of an Imperial statesman to become the assailant of the Catholic name. He has sought to fix an indelible stigma upon your Faith and character. If the torch, which he cast into the country a few weeks since, has been extinguished at a moment's notice, it is due to the common sense of the English people. The various organs of the Press, with the shrewd political sense for which they are conspicuous, without any possible collusion, extinguished its political import in a single morning. Twenty years ago and we should perhaps have been in the midst of the fires of political and civil and social discord. The English people have moved onward, and are willing to form a juster appreciation of you, and to judge you by your lives and conduct. Our thanks are due to those who have quenched the fire, or at least restricted its circuit to almost a theological arena. Little heed can be given to the assurance that it was intended to stop short of penal laws and German persecution. The person who applies a firebrand can prescribe no limits to the conflagration.

The gist of Mr. Gladstone's accusation is as follows:—As Catholics you have surrendered your mental and moral freedom. Your loyalty to the Queen and your civil allegiance are as base coin in false currency; you have made yourselves over to a foreigner who has neither heart nor interest in the British Empire.

You have been wounded by these imputations in your tenderest sense of honour; you have been outraged in your holy religion.

It is right that on such an occasion you should hear your Pastor's voice, and that he should direct your thoughts in the way of peace and truth.

II.—OUR GENERAL PRINCIPLES ON ALLEGIANCE.

The precise meaning of the word "allegiance" is nowhere given in Mr. Gladstone's pamphlet. It was perhaps more convenient to leave it vague. For ourselves, however, we prefer to define our terms. Allegiance, then, we understand to be the subject's duty of fidelity to his Sovereign. The allegiance of man in its absolute, unrestricted, and universal extent is due to his Sovereign Creator alone. The Creator having compounded him of matter and of spirit, having of his free love given him a spiritual and a heavenly as well as a civil and a natural life and end, and having fashioned him to live in society, in the very nature of things placed him under the authority of two Powers—one Spiritual and one Civil. These two Powers from the beginning were essentially distinct; but through the corruption of man at the fall, the natural and Civil Power became satisfied with nothing less than domination. It grasped possession of the Spiritual Power, and either incorporated it into itself, or, keeping it nominally distinct, held it as a subject and an instrument of the State. On the other hand, as a witness against this outrage, God was pleased to give to his chosen race a Theocracy—in which, however, the two Powers were preserved with a sufficient distinctness to mark the principle. When the King of Kings became incarnate, and determined to establish on earth the Spiritual Kingdom, which had been announced by his Prophets, He drew once more, absolutely and definitely, the distinction and separation between these two Powers— "Render to Cæsar the things that are Cæsar's, and to God the things that are God's." When this solemn message of radical reform by the King of Kings was carried from the obscure province of Palestine to the Emperors of Rome, they treated it first with scorn, then with fear, and lastly with hatred and persecution;

"Who is this, they cried with fury, that He should invade our domain, that He should attempt to parcel out that which is indivisible, giving over the care and administration of material and earthly affairs to us, and reserving to himself the care and government of the souls of men and of religion?"

For three hundred years they endeavoured, with the aid of all their resources, to stamp out the very notion of such a division, by steadily, century after century, putting to death the Vicar of that foreign King, scattering his subjects, with repeated declarations that the Christian religion was incompatible with the State; whilst, on the other hand, every effort was made to rehabilitate and confirm the theory of the universal authority of the Civil Power.

The doctrine of the King of Kings triumphed, and that of the Pagan world perished—perished in Christendom for over a thousand years. Those who have lived in Rome will remember the famous Arch of Constantine. The historian Eusebius somewhere tells us that under his statue, holding in the right hand the standard of the Cross, Constantine had written these words—" By this saving Sign, the true token of strength, I have freed your city from the yoke of tyranny, have conferred freedom on the Senate and the Roman people, and have restored Rome to its pristine greatness and splendour." The freedom of the human race, in intellect, will, and moral nature, was guaranteed by the distinction laid down by Jesus Christ. He had come truly and in every sense to be our Saviour and to set men free. The deep and permanent foundations of our public liberty rest upon the jurisdiction of the

Spiritual Power being separate from and independent of that of the State.

There are then established by God, and subject to Him, two Sovereignties, the Spiritual and the Civil. We owe allegiance to both. To talk of our allegiance either to the Civil or to the Spiritual Power as being "divided," leads in popular language to misunderstanding; and does not appear correct. To say that we pay a "divided allegiance" is as though we were to say that we paid a "divided debt," or performed a "divided act of mercy." And to assert of a wife that she pays a "divided" allegiance to her husband would suggest suspicion. Allegiance is due to each power within its own order or province. That which is one is not divisible or divided, and the two Orders of Power, as set up by God, are not antagonisms but harmonies, as God designed them. Only the sin of man can create a conflict. In intensity and degree our civil allegiance, whether to a Sovereign person or to a Sovereign body, is without limit in its own order. We must lay down our life in its service when required. We must be faithful to it unto death.

The *duty* of the civil allegiance of the subject is co-extensive with the *right* of the Sovereign,—to which it is the correlative. The *civil duty* of the subject, therefore, is limited only by the *civil right* of the Sovereign. But the Sovereign who reigns for a civil end, has no right or power over spiritual or divine Laws. He is himself subject to them, and must obey them like the least of his people; he will be judged by them, and punished or rewarded eternally, according to the sentence of the Just Judge.

The allegiance we owe to the Spiritual Sovereignty is also in intensity and degree without limit in its own order, but it is of another and of a pre-eminent order to the Civil. We must suffer any penalty, even that of death, rather than be faithless to this allegiance.

The domain of the Spiritual Sovereignty is the Spiritual life of man, and whatever is directly and essentially connected with it. It has the ultimate interpretation and guardianship of the Moral and Divine Law. Being of a pre-eminent and higher order, being spiritual, having received under the new dispensation a special commission from God, and with its awful purposes and end stretching out into eternity, it is supreme, able to define its own limits, and the necessary conditions of its healthy life and action. The rest belongs to the natural and civil order. These two Sovereignties in their normal state—as God would have them working together in harmony, like all the works of His hand,—are necessary to one another and supplementary of one another; and hence the Vicar of Christ condemned with infallible precision this proposition, "The Church should be separated from the State, and the State from the Church." (*Syllabus*, Prop. lv.) Where the world has altogether departed from the ordinance of God, and the discord of Babel prevails in religious matters, it is evident that we are in an abnormal condition. This is the condition of modern society, and hence the application of the doctrine of the union of Church and State must be determined in practice by existing circumstances. Never, however, can a Christian accept, either in theory or in practice, the subjugation of the Spiritual to the Civil Sovereignty. For this truth, our Catholic forefathers in this country suffered persecution for 300 years; and the Nonconformists equally preferred the penalty of civil disabilities rather than acquiesce in the dependence of the Spiritual upon the Civil Authority.

2. The question now arises, *In what does the Spiritual Power consist? In whom or in what is it embodied and made sensible to us?* This is the question at the bottom of Mr. Gladstone's pamphlet; yet with the wonted dexterity of a practised debater he eludes, and even entirely conceals it from the public view.

The Spiritual Power in the world, to which all are called upon to submit, is undoubtedly that which is the appointed supreme Guardian and Interpreter of the moral and the Divine law of God. To this proposition all assent.

But *who*, or *what*, is that supreme Guardian and Interpreter? This, as we have said, is the real point at issue. Logically and theologically Mr. Gladstone was first of all bound to settle this. He has nominally addressed his pamphlet to Catholics, and has ignored this which is the first principle and basis of their life and conduct. He has assumed a premise which is neither proved nor granted, trusting to the sympathy of public prejudice. But all conclusions fall to pieces as worthless which are not drawn out of true and living premises.

There are four different theories which profess to answer this primary and fundamental question, "Who is the Supreme Guardian and Interpreter of the moral and Divine Law? Where is the Spiritual Power?"

(1). The first is the old **pagan** or modern **Erastian**,

which invests its guardianship and interpretation in the Civil Authority.

(2). The second is the theory put forward by the rationalist and semi-rationalist school, and it would seem to be also that of Mr. Gladstone ; viz.: the private conscience and reason of each individual.

(3). The third is the old Protestant theory of the Divine Authority of the Bible without note or comment.

(4). The fourth is that of a Divine Teacher speaking with an audible and living voice, easily accessible to men, able to expound its meaning, and capable of dealing with the difficult spiritual problems which are bred of the multiform combinations of our perpetually shifting times and circumstances.

It is unnecessary for the moment to do more than mention the first of these theories as the pagan and German system, which having a prophet in London, is making a slow but steady growth in England.

Upon the second, Fetishism and the most monstrous idolatries are defensible; it may be pleaded as a justification of rebellion, communism, and of every theory that, springing from the fevered brain of man, has carried off conscience and reason to obey its behests. It is the plea put forward by every political assassin, and is the defence set up for every crime committed (in the name of religion) with cold and deliberate forethought.

As to the third, it may suffice to say that in principle it is indeed an appeal to an external authority and to a Divine Teacher, though in practice it is the doctrine of private judgment. *Quot homines tot sententiæ.*

The fourth theory is that which was held by Christendom undividedly for fifteen centuries; which was professed in England for a thousand years, and is maintained to this day by 200,000,000, or one-fifth of the human race. It is a theory, therefore, entitled to respectful consideration. It cannot be elbowed out of court, as it lately has been, as though it had no right to be heard or even to be present. This theory is easily stated, and may be put as follows.

III.—A Divine Teacher Claims the Reasonable Submission of Our Mental and Moral Nature.

1. This is our Catholic belief. Human reason and conscience, since the fall, have stood in constant need of a Spiritual Power which shall be a Divine Teacher. Human teachers have not sufficed: they are blind leaders of the blind. We refuse unconditional submission to any of them. The Catholic holds it a degradation and a crime to give over his reason or his conscience into the hands of any man. These, like the priceless treasure of a man's own consciousness, are sacred, inviolate, and inalienable. But if, on the one hand, he may not part with his conscience or reason, on the other, the experience of six thousand years, including the periods of civilization of the four great Empires of antiquity, has proved to demonstration the weakness, the blindness, and the folly of human reason and conscience in all that concerns the law of God, when cut adrift from the light and guidance of an Eternal and Divine Teacher. The hopeless wreck at this moment of at least three-fourths of the human family

beyond the pale of Christendom, sunk in every kind of abominable vice and error, and the chaotic confusion of a hundred sects within its pale, are evidence to every thoughtful and dispassionate mind of the absolute necessity of a Divine Teacher.

As a matter of fact, God never did from the beginning of the world abandon the human race to the guidance and care of reason without the external aid of a Divine Authority. The Divine Teacher was in the world from Adam through the Patriarchs to Moses, and from Moses through Priests and Prophets to the time of Christ.

It is a doctrine of our Faith that reason and conscience, aided by grace, will lead a man, if faithful to both, to see the necessity of a Divine Teacher. Having arrived at this, they will lead him further: they will convince him that the Divine Teacher can be no other than the Catholic Church.

If Mr. Gladstone's study and reading, if Mr. Gladstone's reason and conscience have not led him to this conclusion ; if no inkling of this truth has ever dawned upon his soul, and if he has not fatally dallied with the calls of grace, then must he, and all who are like him, be reputed free from the *blame* of error and from the formal sin of misbelief. We, as Catholics, are far from condemning all men who differ from ourselves, though we may know them to be misguided ; we shall all be judged before a just tribunal ; we leave the judgment to Almighty God.

But what we deny with all the energy of our soul is this, that either Mr. Gladstone or any man, who respects the sanctity of conscience and the light of reason, can consistently charge with the "forfeiture of mental and moral freedom" those who, having found a Divine Teacher, have become His faithful and devoted children.

When the fisherman of Galilee in the joy of his heart cried out, "We have found the Messias" (*Jo.* i. 41), he called to his brethren, "Come and see." He began to form his reason and conscience upon the life and teaching of his new Master. Who will reproach him with having abandoned his mental and moral freedom, or with having jeopardised his civil allegiance? It matters little, brethren, whether it be a Jew or a Gentile, a fisherman or a politician; when once he has found the Divine Teacher he must become His faithful disciple. The light of truth is the freedom of reason and conscience: and the office of the Divine Teacher is to teach us truth of the moral and supernatural order. Whoever asserts that to follow such a One is to "forfeit mental and moral freedom" is a blasphemer, and the truth is not in him. But it will be urged, in reply, that the writer of the pamphlet nowhere affirms that to submit to a *Divine* Teacher is to forfeit mental and moral freedom: his charge is, that submission to the Catholic Church involves that forfeiture. In other words, as we have said, he has *assumed* (1) that the Catholic Church is not a Divine Teacher, and (2) that there exists no *living* Divine Teacher of the law of God in the world.

IV.—OUR DIVINE LORD'S PRINCIPLE AND PLAN OF TEACHING.

1. Note well the plan of our Lord's teaching; see

the order in which He began. He first sought to win from His hearers a belief in His Divine Authority. It was for this purpose that He wrought His miracles. He showed himself as the Divine Teacher. "Never did *man* speak like this man" (*Jo.* vii. 46). "He taught as one having authority" (*Matt.* vii. 29). He taught His disciples to accept His doctrines, not because they commended themselves to human reason (*Jo.* vi. 61–9, xiv. 12), but upon faith in Him as the Divine Teacher.

Now, note well the principle underlying His entire system. It is in radical opposition to modern rationalism and private judgment. Christ's first undertaking was to convince His hearers that He was a Divine Teacher, with a claim to absolute submission. Everything was to hinge on this admission. Until this claim to AUTHORITY on the one hand and corresponding OBEDIENCE on the other was settled, nothing was taught or believed, nothing effected. He established this claim by addressing a great variety and number of proofs to their reason and common sense, whilst at the same time he proclaimed the absolute necessity of grace, preaching penance, and declaring that "no one could come to Him unless the Father drew him." He proved His Divine Authority (1) by miracles [*]; (2) by prophecies uttered by Himself and afterwards fulfilled, and by His knowledge of secret thoughts [†]; (3) by the fulfilment in His own person of the prophecies

---

[*] *Matt.* xi. 5; *Jo.* x. 37; xv. 24; xi. 42, &c. The chief end of St. John's Gospel was to prove the Divinity by miracles; see c. xx. 30, 31.

[†] *Matt.* xxiv.; *Luke* xviii. 31, &c.; *Jo.* ii. 19; xii. 32, &c.; xiv. 29, &c.; *Jo.* i. 48; ii. 24, 25; xiii. 18.

of the Old Testament *; (4) by His transfiguration and the appearance of Moses and Elias, witnessed by three of His apostles †; (5) by the whole character and tenor of his life and conduct; (6) by that climax of proof which confirmed the certainty already created, viz., His Resurrection to life, which was proved to demonstration by His apparitions to all classes of men at different seasons, and (7) finally by His admirable Ascension. The accumulation of proof was overwhelming. Still without grace no man could become a Christian. In proportion as belief in Him as a Divine Teacher was established during the course of His ministry, in that proportion did He reveal His various doctrines. Hence He taught more truths to the Apostles than to the disciples or the multitudes; and He went on progressively even with the Apostles, revealing more sublime mysteries and adding to the number of truths communicated, as they advanced in a firm and rooted belief in Himself as their Divine Teacher. He thus laid the ground or basis of supernatural Faith, viz.: belief in the claim of a Divine Teacher. Observe this, moreover, that He left none of His Divine Truths to be accepted or not according to preference, choice, caprice, or private judgment and reason. His followers must either be with Him *entirely*, or leave Him. There was no " mental and moral freedom " to be urged against the claims of a Divine Teacher. They were free to go away and they were free to stay; but not free to stay with Him *and* at the same time to disbelieve Him (Jo.

---

* *Matt.* xxvi. 54: *Luke* xxiv. 25, &c.; *Jo.* v. 39, 46; *Matt.* v. 17; *Luke* xvi. 16; *Jo.* i. 17; cfr. *Gal.* iii. 23, iv. 4; *Eph.* i 10.

† *Matt.* iii. 16: xvii. 2; *Jo.* xii. 28; *II. Pet.* i. 16, &c.

vi.) Each doctrine was to be accepted by mind and heart, with the entire soul, not because it commended itself to *reason* (though it could never *contradict* reason), or to the feelings, or to the refined taste of culture, or to worldly happiness, or to political expediency. No other motive of credibility or submission was put forward or allowed but that of the authority and veracity of the Divine Teacher. Having thus laid down the basis of Faith, He expounded His doctrines; and then provided for their permanent and unbroken tradition through future ages by founding a Church which was to be their Guardian and Interpreter.

V.—His Church founded as a Divine Teacher on the same Principle and Plan.

The Church founded by Christ is an organisation composed of a Divine and human element. The human element falls under the cognisance of the senses, and by its perceptible presence the Church becomes a visible institution. Under the human and visible is contained the other element which is Divine. Such is your Faith as to the component parts of the Church.

1. Let us now inquire upon what grounds the Church is described as a *Divine* Teacher, whom all are called upon to obey. *First,* because Christ Himself founded its visible constitution. He created it a true and perfect Society or Kingdom, distinct from the Civil Power and independent of it, with full authority in the triple order (as needful for a perfect kingdom)—legislative, judicial, and coercive. He was Himself the King (*Luke* xxiii. 3). When He withdrew to His

throne above, the constitution remained behind intact. He left a visible Vicar in His place, to be, like Himself, the centre of unity and jurisdiction, to rule and govern, to feed and teach in His name to the end of time.*

2. *Second*, because Christ was the Founder not only of its constitution and external form, but also of the inward principle upon which it should move and act; that is to say, the relation it was to enter into with the human reason and will. He thus endowed the Church with the same Divine teaching authority which He possessed Himself, and exacted from all men a corresponding obedience to its teaching, just as though it spoke with His own sacred lips.

He spoke of *it* precisely as though it were *Himself*. This is seen (1) in the remarkable fact that the severest threats pronounced by our Lord against the disobedient in Faith were uttered not against those who refused to receive the words that fell from His own lips, but from the lips of His Church. "He that despiseth *you* despiseth Me." "If a man will not hear the *Church*, let him be to thee as a heathen;" he that believeth not the Church's preaching shall be condemned (*Matt.* xviii. 17, *Luke* x. 16, *Mark* xvi. 16).

It would appear as though Jesus Christ looked upon Himself as (what He was indeed) the *extraordinary* Divine Teacher, but upon the Church as the Divine Teacher in *ordinary*. He was therefore mild in His threats upon those disobedient to Himself during the years of His ministry, but terribly explicit in

* Matt. xvi. 18, 19; Luke xxii. 31, 32; John xxi. 15, 16, 17.

His denunciation of all who should disobey that Divine Teacher which He founded and endowed, as we shall see, and then sent to accompany mankind through the centuries.

It is (2) abundantly clear that the Apostles thoroughly understood their Lord's meaning, and exercised the right of the teaching authority with which He had invested His Church. This comes out in nearly all their writings. For instance: " We have the mind of Christ." " For Christ we are ambassadors, God, as it were, exhorting by us." " *We* are God's coadjutors, you are God's husbandry, you are God's building." " We have received grace and apostleship for obedience to the Faith in all nations." " Though an angel from heaven preach a gospel to you besides that which *we* have preached, let him be anathema." (I. Cor. ii. 16, II. Cor. v. 20, I. Cor. iii. 9, Rom. i. 5, Gal. i. 8, Rom. x. 14, xv. 18, I. Tim. i. 11, Acts i. 8, xv. 7, 8, &c.)

A distinction is to be borne in mind—the Divine Teacher, Christ, revealed his *own* doctrines, whereas the Divine Teacher, His Church, *makes* no revelation, but guards and interprets with infallible truth the doctrines revealed by her Founder. "You shall be my *witnesses* unto the uttermost parts of the earth " (Acts i. 8).

This fundamental principle established by our Lord as the fit and only relation to exist between the Divine Teacher and mankind continues as it began to this day. The Lord did not start upon one system and break off into another. He did not begin upon the principle of Divine Authority on the one side and of the "obedience of Faith" on the other, and then substitute for Divine Authority human reason and human conscience, and bid every man do that which should seem good to him in his own sight. The Lord is not like to the fickle people that tries on first one system of government, then another; to-day a monarchy, to-morrow an empire, and the day after a republic. The lines upon which He built His system and His Church are permanent, as is proved from Scripture, reason, and tradition.

And now look through all the various systems and forms of worship which torment Christendom, and say in which of them is found the perpetuation of the outward Constitution and of the inward principle we have referred to. So far from being accepted the principle of obedience of Faith to a living Divine Teacher is everywhere rejected with horror, and a favourite statesman of the world denounces it as "the forfeiture of mental and moral freedom." The Catholic Church therefore alone presents to a rebellious world the character and credentials of the Church of Jesus and of the Apostles.

3. *Next*, the Church is Divine not only from having received from her Founder a Commission of Authority which is altogether of a superhuman and divine character, but she is Divine by her twofold divine, essential and constituent element; viz:—(1) the perpetual presence of CHRIST Himself with her teaching and baptizing not merely during the apostolic age but "*all days even to the consummation of the world*" (Matt. xxviii. 20, cfr. Jo. xx. 21, Mark xvi. 15, 16; Matt. xvi. 17, 18, 19, Acts i. 8); and (2) "the abi

ding" habitation within her of the HOLY GHOST. "I will ask the Father, and He shall give you another Paraclete, that He may *abide with you for ever*, the Spirit of Truth" (Jo. xiv. 16, cfr. Jo. xiv. 26, xvi. 13)

You will not fail to observe, dear brethren, how instinct the Church was from the very beginning with the consciousness of possessing, literally, substantially and efficiently these two Divine elements; how her belief was absolute and unshakable in these two stupendous promises made by her Divine Founder—that He Himself would continue WITH her teaching, and that the Holy Spirit of Truth should "COME and ABIDE WITH her FOR EVER."

See too how the early Church fixed its mind upon the inseparable union of this "Divine" *with* the "human" element. Take first the direct and personal relationship of the Church with Christ. It was years after His ascent into Heaven that the Apostle was insisting again and again on this fact :—" Christ is Head over all the Church, which is His body and the fulness of Him" (Eph. c. i.). Again, " Christ is Head of the Church ; He is the Saviour of His body. . . He loved the Church and delivered Himself up for it, that He might sanctify it, cleansing it by the laver of water in the word of life, that He might present it to Himself, a glorious Church not having spot or wrinkle, or any such thing, but that it should be holy and without blemish. . . No man hateth his own flesh, but nourisheth and cherisheth it, as also Christ doth the Church, because we are members of His body, of His flesh, and of His bones" (c. v.) (*Cfr.* Col. i. 18; Eph. iv. 4-5 I. Tim. iii. 15 : Jo. x. 16, &c., &c.)

4. And *lastly*, take the relationship of the Church with the Holy Ghost, as described in the authentic history of the Church. From the day of Pentecost she has been full and overflowing with the consciousness of His Divine presence "abiding WITH her," and that "FOR EVER." Christ had distinctly and frequently promised that He would send the Person of the Holy Spirit after His Ascension. And then, lo! the Holy Ghost came ten days after the Ascension, (Acts ii. 2; Jo. vii. 38-9; xiv. 16; xv. 26; xvi. 7, 12). He came to discharge His mission (1) of teacher; (2) of strengthener and (3) of sanctifier through a mode of habitation. With Him came into the Church the fulness of infallibility in teaching truth, the power of the seven sacraments, and the permanence of the mysteries of grace and sanctity. What the visible presence of Christ had been to the Apostles, that after the day of Pentecost was the Holy Spirit to be to the Church, not for three years, but to the end of time. He was our Lord's Successor, but His dispensation was more glorious. Hence, if you read the history of the Church after the Feast of Pentecost, as recorded in the Acts of the Apostles, you will be struck with the natural way in which the Holy Ghost is mentioned just in the places and at the times and in the manner in which our Blessed Lord is mentioned in the Gospel. "They were all filled with the Holy Ghost" (Acts ii. 4 iv. 31). "Peter said, why hath Satan tempted thy heart to lie to the Holy Ghost?" (Acts v. 3). "Why have you agreed together to tempt the Spirit of the Lord?" (Acts v. 9). "Look ye out seven men full of the Holy Ghost" (Acts vi. 3). "Stephen, a man full

of the Holy Ghost" (Acts vi. 5). "You always resist the Holy Ghost" (Acts vii. 51). "He being filled with the Holy Ghost, looked up steadfastly to them" (Acts vii. 55). "They prayed for them, that they might receive the Holy Ghost" (Acts viii. 15). "They laid hands upon them, and they received the Holy Ghost" Acts viii. 17). "Brother Saul, be filled with the Holy Ghost" (Acts ix. 17). "The Church walking in the fear of the Lord, and filled with the consolations of the Holy Ghost" (Acts ix. 31). "The Holy Ghost fell on all them that hear the word" (Acts x. 44). . . .
"The grace of the Holy Ghost was poured out upon the Gentiles also" (Acts x. 45). "The Holy Ghost fell on them as on us in the beginning" (Acts xi. 15). "You shall be baptized with the Holy Ghost" (Acts xi. 15, 16). "The Holy Ghost said to them, separate me Saul and Barnabas. . . So they being sent by the Holy Ghost, went to Seleucia" (Acts xiii. 2, 4). "And the disciples being filled with joy and the Holy Ghost" (Acts xiii. 52). "God . . . giving unto them the Holy Ghost as well as to us" (Acts xv. 8). "It hath seemed good to the Holy Ghost and to us" (Acts xv. 28). "They were forbidden by the Holy Ghost to preach the word in Asia" (Acts xvi. 6). "And when Paul had imposed hands on them, the Holy Ghost came upon them" (Acts xix. 6). "The Holy Ghost witnesseth in every city to me, saying, &c." (Acts xx. 23). So impressed was the early Church with this truth of the *abiding* presence of the Holy Spirit, that St. Peter declares to Ananias and Sapphira that in telling a lie to him as head of the Church" (Acts v. 3), "they had lied to the Holy Ghost." And at the

General Council of Jerusalem, over which St. Peter presided, the decree passed seemed to run quite naturally in these words:—" It hath seemed good to the Holy Ghost and to us" (Acts xv. 28). And when St. Paul was about to leave the Bishops of Ephesus, he said to them, " take heed to yourselves and to the whole flock over which the *Holy Spirit* hath placed you Bishops to rule the Church of God" (Acts xx. 28).

The presence of the Holy Ghost in the Church is as heavenly fire in an earthly element. So that the Apostle described the Catholic Church with literal exactness as " one body and one Spirit " (Eph. iv. 4).

It would be easy to quote similar allusions from all the Epistles, if we have not yet learned this truth:— that the Apostles seemed to consider no duty more urgent upon them than to keep perpetually and most prominently before the minds of their followers the presence of a Divine Life, animating the Catholic Church; the *human* element seems to pass almost out of mind in the reiterated insistance upon the claim of the Divine.

VI.—THE ROMAN CATHOLIC AND APOSTOLIC CHURCH THE DIVINE TEACHER.

1. A stranger may fairly inquire for the marks whereby he may know the Church to be the Divine Teacher. It would certainly be to do violence to his reason to call upon him to submit to her authority without convincing proof of her claim to his obedience; and this fact the Church so thoroughly recognizes that she permits no Priest to receive a convert

into the Church unless he is satisfied that he has been *convinced* of her right to his submission. So guarded is the Church on this score, that no Priest can admit an adult into the Church without a *special faculty* from his Bishop for that purpose. And if any one has had experience of the practice in Rome, he will know, perhaps to the cost of his patience, the number of formalities (we believe five in number) to be gone through and of permissions from different quarters to be obtained, before a convert can be admitted into the Church. People judging superficially would say that Rome thus actually puts difficulties into the way of conversion, instead of grasping for converts, as men say she does. The reason of all this is, that the Church must satisfy herself that the catechumen has been *reasonably convinced* of her Divine character. Has the Church, then, any marks whereby you may know her to be the Divine Teacher; and if so, what are they? She has her marks, just as Jesus Christ had His marks. We have already, in an earlier part of this letter, briefly referred to the marks or proofs which our Lord considered sufficient to convince the Jews of His claim to their submission; we must now refer to those of the Church with equal brevity. Your Catechism mentions them most compendiously. "She is One, she is Holy, she is Catholic, and she is Apostolical." Bellarmine gives fifteen marks whereby the reason may be convinced of the authority of the Church. But, you may object that men will deny her marks one after the other. But they equally denied the marks offered by our Lord of His Divinity, one after the other. They denied His most conspicuous mark or character, that of sanctity: saying by "Beelzebub He casteth out devils;" He "hath a devil;" He is a "blasphemer," a "deceiver," a "liar," a "sinner:" —the Civil Power even attempted to deny His resurrection, and said that the disciples had stolen away His body whilst the soldiers slept. Be not astonished, therefore, if men deny the proofs of the authority of the Church of God, since they denied the proofs of the authority of Christ. But bear this further point well in mind. You have need to do so: the proofs or marks, though they address themselves to the reason and conscience, will never inspire Divine Faith unless "the Father" also " draw " them*—" Faith is a gift of God."

2. We can add only one further word on this part of our subject—viz., that the proofs of the Divine character of the Church are more luminous even than those of the Divinity of Christ, because we have, *plus* those of His Divinity (and therefore of His power and veracity), the experience of the fulfilment of His promises to His Church. The history of eighteen centuries of plotting against the Church and of persecution of every kind on the part of the powers of hell and of the world for the purpose of destroying that sacred edifice which He built upon a Rock, is the strongest historical proof of her Divine origin. And if to the evidence of the history of persecution without, you add the history of her life within—the exemplary and unbroken succession of her Pontiffs, the fruits of her sacraments, of her teaching and direction in the saints of every age, her martyrs, her miracles, and even the temporal benefits

---

* *Jo.* vi. 44; *Eph.* ii. 8.

she has scattered among men, as with queenly grace she proceeds upon her Divine and Spiritual mission,—you will have a *cumulus* of historical proof such as the Christians of the early Church had nothing to compare with, and without which they still became converts, and gladly laid down their lives as a testimony.

The history of the Catholic Church is a fact at least as credible as the history of the world, and its history corroborates the perpetual existence of his *Divine* as well as of its *human* component. Taking in thus the testimony of history, we may say, only with greater precision of Catholicity, that which Butler's *Analogy* (Part II. ch. vii.) says of Christianity, that its evidence is " a long series of things, reaching, as it seems, from the beginning of the world to the present time, of great variety and compass, taking in both the direct and the collateral proofs, and making up all of them together one argument; the conviction arising from which kind of proof may be compared to what they call *the effect* in architecture or other works of art; a result from a great number of things so and so disposed and taken into one view." The evidences for the claim of the Catholic Church to our submission are therefore greater and more numerous to-day than they were when it first issued forth from the Upper Chamber in the morning of the Descent of the Holy Ghost.

VII.—INFALLIBILITY OF THE DIVINE TEACHER.

1 —It is furthermore clear to us that this Church, this Divine Society, this Spiritual Kingdom, created by Christ and ordained to last to the end of the world,

and to claim the submission of every soul must—in order to accomplish her work without violation of the human reason and conscience,—possess not only a Divine authority, but the endowment also of a teaching infallibility in Faith and Morals.

Look around you, brethren, and see who lay claim to possession of this gift; positively there is not one but the Roman Catholic and Apostolic Church. She alone claims it as her Divine prerogative.

For 1800 years and more has she taught the doctrine of her supreme authority and doctrinal infallibility; but never till the Vatican Council did she *define* her infallibility by a *dogmatic decree*. And wherefore this strange long *absence* of a definition of her fundamental character? For the same reason that the decree passed in the first Council of Jerusalem, occurs in the fifteenth chapter of the Book of *Acts*, and not in the second or the third; that is to say, for this simple reason, that the Church makes her decrees and definitions according to times and circumstances; or, in other words, according to the need. She had never defined her infallibility before the Vatican Council, because never had a Catholic, even a Gallican, denied it. Wherefore, then, its definition at the Vatican Council? Because of a local and transient error, touching the *condition*, not of its existence, but of its exercise. That error maintained that the definitions of the Sovereign Pontiff are indeed infallible, but only after *subjection* to the assent of the Episcopate. This was the Gallican phase of error, which under royal patronage received a form in 1682, and was adhered to by some 33 or 34 Bishops convened by Louis XIV. out of over a hundred of the French Episcopate. It was at once treated as an error; but it lingered locally, under the patient toleration (*not* approval) of the Pontiffs, till the meeting of the General Council. It was then expunged for ever by a dogmatic decree on Infallibility. That decree, as you are aware, was made by the Pope in General Council (the largest but one ever held) and it is therefore, even upon the most extreme of Gallican theories, binding upon every Catholic, under pain of heresy and damnation. The Catholic Church, then, has once more been declared the Divine Teacher of the world, by the Definition of the Infallibility of her Visible Head.

2. And now, brethren, very briefly, as to the extent of ground covered by the Vicar of Christ's infallibility in Faith and Morals. It is defined that the ground is co-extensive with that covered by the infallibility of the Church herself. It is of Catholic and Divine Faith (that is to say, it is a term of Catholic communion) that it includes the whole deposit of Revelation; and, according to the teaching of theologians, it is theologically certain (and can be also held, as we ourselves hold it, to be of Faith), that it includes all those unrevealed truths which so touch on the deposit of Faith as that Faith and Morals cannot be guarded and infallibly interpreted without an infallible discernment of such truths.

The following is the Definition of the Council:

"Wherefore, faithfully adhering to the tradition received from the beginning of the Christian Faith, for the glory of God our Saviour, the exaltation of the Catholic religion, and the salvation of Christian people, the Sacred Council approving,—we teach and define that it is a dogma divinely revealed, that the Roman

Pontiff when he speaks *ex cathedrâ*,—that is, when in discharge of the office of Pastor and Doctor of all Christians by virtue of his Supreme Apostolic authority, he defines a doctrine regarding Faith or morals to be held by the Universal Church—by the divine assistance promised to him in Blessed Peter, is possessed of that infallibility with which the divine Redeemer willed that His Church should be endowed for defining doctrine regarding Faith or morals: and, therefore, such definitions of the Roman Pontiff are irreformable of themselves, and not from the consent of the Church.

" And if anyone—which may God avert—presume to contradict this our definition; let him be anathema."

3. As a term of communion, this definition must be interpreted strictly and literally, and, as you will perceive, it refers only to Definitions *ex cathedrâ;* that is to say, it does not include the Pope's utterances as a private Doctor, his opinions as a theologian, or the exercise of his directive, discretionary, and administrative authority in the affairs of individuals or of the Church at large. It refers solely to (1) solemn definitions of *Doctrine;* (2) regarding Faith or Morals; (3) uttered by virtue of his supreme Apostolic authority; (4) in discharge of the office of Pastor and Doctor of all Christians; and (5) with the intention of binding the Universal Church. Bear this definition and its conditions well in mind and you will be able to answer at once nearly all objectors. It is not hard to believe that Jesus Christ, having confided His entire Flock to the care of Peter, should have "confirmed *his* faith" for the sake of the Flock: rather would it be hard to believe that

He had left him without a "divine assistance' in the midst of the powers of earth and hell.

O Vicar of Jesus Christ on earth! thou art then our incomparable Shepherd-King, our Priest and Prophet. The care of the entire Flock of Christ is upon thy soul. On thy placid brow is the triple crown of Charity, Truth, and Power. Upon thy shoulder rest the keys of Heaven. Of all kings, thou alone art by right Divine the first, the highest, and the oldest. All are thy subjects * within the order over which thou rulest. They may despoil thee of thy earthly trappings, but they can never uncrown thee. They may close upon thee as a prisoner, but they can never reduce thee to their subjection.

4. Be not deceived, dear brethren and children, be not deceived. It is not the Church as a congregation that the world hates with a fiendish hatred. It is not this or that or the other doctrine—the Immaculate Conception, the Invocation of Saints, the Holy Mass, or the Seven Sacraments. The real gravamen is not in these. It is the perpetual presence of a Divine Teacher, teaching with authority and infallibility; preaching penance to a sinful world lest it should perish in eternal flames; rebuking error in every form, as the faithful Guardian of the Law of God.

The Vicar of Christ stands up to the world as Elias

* A king is "*subjectus ratione peccati*, not *ratione dominii*," as Boniface VIII. says, *i.e.*, the morality of all acts, political no less than private, are subject to the Supreme Judge and Guardian of the Divine law. The same Pope also says, " in nullo volumus usurpare jurisdictionem regis," cfr. the Bulls *Ausculta, Fili*, and *Unam Sanctam ;* also cfr. *Hist. of Church*, by Döllinger, vol. iv., and *Introd. Lect. on Mod. Hist., Lect.* v., by Dr. T. Arnold.

"stood up" to Achab. "*I* have not troubled Israel," said Elias, "but *thou* and thy father's house who have forsaken the commandments of the Lord" (III. Kings xviii. 18). He corrects and rebukes it for its transgressions as the Baptist condemned the King. The world may call him, as it called Paul, "a pestilent man and raising seditions" (Acts xxiv. 5); it may cast him and those who are with him, like Peter, into prison, for their allegiance to their Divine Redeemer. This is *precisely* our Lord's forewarning. It is *precisely* on account of your *spiritual allegiance* that "they will lay hands on you and persecute you; delivering you up to synagogues and into prisons; *dragging you before kings and governors for My sake*" (Luke xxi. 12.)

And our Lord added encouragement to the prophecy—"This shall happen unto you for a testimony"—a testimony to the Law of God, and for a crown of eternal life. Wonder not, therefore, if men hate the Vicar of Christ. It is meet they should; they smote Jesus on the cheek and called Him *seditious*, a *blasphemer*, and *possessed by devils;* they crucified Him for His *teaching on the allegiance* due respectively to the Spiritual and Civil Power.

5. And now, dear brethren and children in Christ, we must add a word, which saddens our heart. A heresy has been set up against the Vatican Council, as one was set up against every other Council that the Church has held. It is that of the little sect of Döllingerites, which takes its name from its unhappy founder. As plants are propagated by slips, so has the heresy been brought to England by a slip taken from the parent plant. It is well known that one object of

Mr. Gladstone's pamphlet was to create division among English Catholics and to stimulate the growth of the new heresy. Some three or four Catholics have responded by name to his melancholy invitation. Their names are familiar to us all as having once and again on former occasions spoken in the spirit of rebellion against the Church's authority or her definitions. Only one of these was in any way a spiritual subject of our jurisdiction, and towards him we have acted as it became our duty. Meanwhile we make known to you, beloved children in Jesus Christ, who are our joy, because among you we know of none who has renounced his faith, that any person, be he of high or of low degree, impiously denying the doctrine of the Immaculate Conception of our dear and ever Blessed Virgin Mother, or the definitions of the Vatican Council, has made shipwreck of the Faith, is excommunicated from the Church of God, incapable of receiving the Holy Sacraments, even in the hour of death, unless previously he truly repent in his heart, and promise to repair, as far as he may be able, the scandal which he has given.

VIII.—SOME COUNTS OF ACCUSATION.

1. We have hitherto dwelt upon the *Divine* element of the Church. She has also a *human* one. And unless we look this fact well in the face, we shall not be able (1) to give a complete answer to the charge of hostility to mental freedom which Mr. Gladstone has brought against the Church of God, or (2) to expose the worthlessness of the objections raised against infallibility, by

those who collect and catalogue the human sins and errors of some of her children.

First, then, with regard to the charge of mental slavery brought against the Catholic Church, in reference to the truths of religion; for as the natural sciences are not her domain, we need not touch upon her relation to these, further than to say that her children are absolutely free to study them, guided by this self-evident principle, that facts in science can never conflict with revealed truths, and that no theories can be accepted as scientifically true which are clearly contrary to the truths of Revelation. Our God is a God of Truth.

From what has been said about authority, it may be inferred by a non-Catholic that the Church crams her teaching down our throats without reason or explanation of any kind. There could not be a greater misapprehension of the fact. Truth can be received only by the intellect, and therefore the Church invites the keenest attention and action of our intellect to her teaching. Reason is not the *motive* of credibility in Divine Faith, but the Veracity of God revealing and of the Church witnessing to the truths of revelation. We stand in absolute need of a Divine Teacher to secure this *motive:* —this is not a gag to reason or conscience. The certainty of Faith is of a higher kind than the certainty of unillumined or mere natural reason.

To those, then, who assert that our obedience to the Church must necessarily restrain and fetter reason, we reply (1) that we never heard that the axioms and rules of Euclid, or the fixed rules of any science, were considered to fetter the intellect or restrain any reasonable freedom of discussion and investigation. And it is precisely the same in the science of religion or theology. The decrees and definitions of the Church are the fixed points, without which there could be no certain science of theology. The liberty which the world pleads for in matters of morality and religion is the liberty to put black for white, and light for darkness, according to the inclination or passion of each one; but this is the license of error and the bondage of confusion.

We reply (2) that no science has ever presented a wider field for study and for the operations of human reason than Catholic philosophy and theology. And no science in the whole course of its career can produce an array of intellectual works to be compared for number and variety, for depth of thought, consistency, argument, and interest, to the theology of the Church. When the world, or any of its sects, can produce a S. Augustine, a S. Thomas, a Suarez, and a Bossuet among the writers upon *their* views of the moral and Divine law, it will be time to ask whether submission of mind and heart to a Divine Teacher is a " surrender of mental and moral freedom." It is matter of history that the study of the Catholic Faith has rapturously engaged the reason and heart of the noblest natures and deepest intellects that the world has ever known. Without the golden rules of *sentire cum Ecclesia* and of submission to her infallible definitions, these intellectual giants would have wandered like comets, and have been lost to the Church and to the world. But, following these two rules there is no one, be he layman or priest, who may not devote, and this with the blessing of the Church, all his powers of intellect, all he resources of his soul, to the examination, elucidation, and development of the truths and mysteries of religion. Nor is there a doctrine taught by the Church on which she does not engage the sublimest intellects of her children. She has no fear of reason. She knows and has defined that Revelation cannot contradict reason, that the truths of the supernatural cannot be in contradiction with those of the natural order.

We reply (3) that the Church has shown her respect for the dignity of human reason by the condemnation of all those theories which, by unduly limiting its power and value, seemed to dishonour and degrade it. She has ever been the jealous guardian of the dignity of human reason.

2. We may here be permitted to make a short digression from the immediate subject of Mr. Gladstone's pamphlet to another, closely connected with it. If we speak of it at all it must be under the heading of the *Human* element of the Church. You know that owing to the Church being compounded of a human as well as of a Divine element, her children often present to the world the spectacle of sins and scandals. One of the twelve Apostles became a thief and a Deicide, and one of the seven Deacons a heresiarch. Differences of smaller moment arose among the Apostles and founders of various churches, as between Paul and Barnabas. In one part of the world you may hear of a nation sunk in corruption, or of a people tinged with rationalism. At times the sins of priests, bishops and even Popes will be a scandal. But none of these human things can shake your faith in an Institution

which is Divine. If they could, it would only prove that you had not based your faith upon its only true and sure foundation.

The Church has been compared to the field sown by "the good man" with wheat, and by "the enemy" with cockle, and to a net gathering in all manner of fishes (*Matt.* xiii.).

Upon this general principle then you will be able to interpret the value of two scandalous letters by Lord Acton, which have been published in *The Times* newspaper in connection with Mr. Gladstone's attack upon the Church. Firstly, then, scandals such as these must come. The noble author assured the world that he was induced to make his historical revelations against S. Pius, Fénélon and others, in the cause of truth. We say nothing of the loyalty or tenderness of a son towards his mother who, upon the occasion of her being grossly and unfairly attacked, should join with her assailants in exposing her frailties. The fact that she possesses an undying life and can bear yet crueller treatment can scarcely mitigate our estimate of the conduct of such a son. He strikes, but professes that he *cannot* kill.

The Times has described the charges brought against saintly members of his Church by Lord Acton, as "overwhelming." The *Pall Mall Gazette* could see only "three courses open to Catholics;" to *refute* them (a task it considered Catholics unequal to), or to *deny* the facts by an act of authority (!), or to *approve* them. There is yet a fourth course possible to one who distinguishes between impeccability and infallibility, and that might be to admit and regret them.

This last course, however, is by no means necessary. We are not ourselves capable of the task of refuting the alleged statements, being neither sufficiently versed in obscure history, nor having the sources of history within our reach. But it appears that the refutation of Lord Acton's various charges is forthcoming.*

Be on your guard, dear brethren, against accepting strange and unknown tales of scandal until they are proved. Ask upon what evidence they rest; whether upon that of eye and ear witnesses, or upon hearsay; whether upon the testimony of men of unimpeachable veracity and disinterestedness, or upon that of intriguers, courtiers, diplomatists, or politicians of more than doubtful character.† Ascertain whether the evidence may not be a forgery or have been tampered with; whether there be not contradictory evidence adducible, which in a Court of justice might cancel the indictment. Let these and similar enquiries be made and answered before you believe in such statements as have been dug out and paraded by Lord Acton.

3. We now pass on to the main practical difficulty which has been suggested to the English people against your allegiance. It is well that you should have an answer to those who question you in good faith.

" What," they say, " if a conflict take place between the Spiritual and Civil Powers—that is, between the

---

* See issues of *Tablet*, Nov. 28, Dec. 5, 12, 19, 26, 1874, especially articles on "Lord Acton's evidence," and a letter signed "E.S.K." "Lord Acton and S. Pius V.," "Lord Acton's proofs," and letters signed " W.B.G.J.," " Canon Toole," &c., &c.

† The Duke of Alva characterized Ridolfi, Lord Acton's trusted authority against S. Pius, as " a great babbler."

Church and the Secular Government?—whom should Catholics then obey?

The reply is clear and categoric. (1.) In the matter of the *Divine Law*, we must obey the Divine Teacher —*i.e.*, the Supreme Guardian and Interpreter of the Divine law. The conflict, alas, has often arisen. It arose between the State and Christ, and the State delivered Him up to death; it arose between His Vicar and Nero, and Nero put him to death; it arose between the Church and the Empire, and lasted for three hundred years, and the Empire regularly for three hundred years put the head of the Church to death; and so on in various times and places down to our day, when the martyrs and confessors of the Church are suffering in the Corea, in Tenquin, and Prussia, in testimony to the supremacy of the moral and divine law. The Church is not the maker, but the guardian and interpreter of these laws. She has no discretion but to declare them. She has no power whatever to abrogate them. She must suffer for them to the death.

(2.) If it be in a matter of *purely ecclesiastical law*, the case is different. The Church has always shown herself ready in every age to come to an understanding with the Civil Power, to relax her purely ecclesiastical laws, and sometimes even to repeal them in conformity with State exigencies. All history bears abundant witness to this, and Mr. Gladstone and every statesman who has studied the history of his own time is without excuse if he does not know it. The civil and international law of Christendom from the fourth century to our own has recognized the power of the Church as a contracting party. Witness the concordats freely entered into at different times with every State in Europe; witness the legates, the nuncios, the plenipotentiaries, and Papal ministers at various Courts. Their mission, their sole *raison d'être*, is to bring about or to continue a mutual, good, and friendly understanding between the Spiritual and Civil Power.

But finally, we are ready to allow that after everything has been said and done, intricacies and entanglements may occasionally occur upon the border land which marks the Spiritual from the Temporal territory. It is so with adjacent States and neighbouring Kingdoms in the same civil order. Human ignorance or human perversity may create a difficulty where the limits meet, and have not been mutually, fully, and clearly agreed upon. To this we reply, that the life and conduct of the Church for eighteen centuries is an ample guarantee for her love of peace and justice. Even where her cause is clearly just, and she cannot without a betrayal of God's cause approve or yield, her appeals are not made to rebellion and the clash of arms, but to the reason and conscience of the human race. Her strength, like that of woman, lies not in physical, but in moral force.

4. Great stress has been laid upon the supposition that the infallibility of the Vicar of Christ forms a political and civil danger.

The Vatican Council, in express words, defines that no *new* prerogative has been made or given. The definition of an *ancient* doctrine,—and Mr. Gladstone himself allows it has been explicitly taught for a thousand years,—cannot create a *new* peril for human society.

Upon this very subject Bishop Milner wrote thus vigorously before the passing of the Act of 1829: —" I was educated in the belief of the Pope's inerrancy. . . But if the layman, who never fails to ridicule the doctrine in question, is willing fairly to contest it, he knows where to meet an antagonist ready to engage with him. Against one assertion, however, of this writer, which insinuates the *political danger resulting* from the doctrine of *Papal* Infallibility, I will hurl defiance at him; nothing being more easy to show, than that no greater danger can result to the State from admitting the *inerrancy of the Pope* than from admitting *that of the Church itself.*"*

But Mr. Gladstone cannot fail to have seen and read the Official Letter Cardinal Antonelli addressed in 1870, in answer to a public Statesman on this very point.

"The subjects (these are the words of the Cardinal) treated of (in the Council) are no more than the exposition of the maxims and fundamental principles of the Church; principles repeated over and over in the acts of former general Councils, proclaimed and developed in several Pontifical Constitutions, published in all Catholic States, and particularly in the celebrated dogmatic Bulls beginning ' *Unigenitus* ' and ' *Auctorem Fidei*,' where all the aforesaid doctrines are generally confirmed and sanctioned; principles finally, which have constantly formed the basis of teaching in all periods of the Church, and in all Catholic Schools, and have been defended by an innumerable host of

---

* " Ecclesiastical Democracy detected."

Ecclesiastical writers, whose works have served for text in public schools and colleges, government schools as well as others, without any contradiction on the part of the civil authority, but rather, for the most part, with the approbation and encouragement of the same." . . .

"The Church has never intended, nor now intends, to exercise any direct or absolute power over the political rights of the State. Having received from God the lofty mission of guiding men, whether individually or as congregated in society, to a supernatural end, she has by that very fact the authority and the duty to judge concerning the morality and justice of all acts, internal and external, in relation to their conformity with the natural and divine law. And as no action, whether it be ordered by a supreme power, or be freely elicited by an individual, can be exempt from this character of morality and justice; so it happens, that the judgment of the Church, though falling directly on the morality of the acts, *indirectly* reaches over everything with which that morality is conjoined. But this is not the same thing as to interfere directly in political affairs, which, by the order established by God and by the teaching of the Church herself, appertains to the *temporal* power *without dependence on any other* authority." . . .

"Whereas no civil society can subsist without a supreme principle regulating the morality of its acts and laws, the Church has received from God this lofty mission, which tends to the happiness of the people, while she in no way embarrasses by the exercise of this her ministry, the free and prompt action of government.

She, in fact, by inculcating the principle of rendering to God that which is God's, and to Cæsar that which is Cæsar's, imposes at the same time upon her children the obligation of obeying the authority of Princes for conscience sake. But these should also recognise that if anywhere a law is made opposed to the principles of eternal justice, to obey would not be a giving to Cæsar that which is Cæsar's, but a taking from God that which is God's."

Another authority, whose words should carry weight, is the late Cardinal Tarquini, a Roman Professor, and canonist of the highest repute, who was employed in the work of the Vatican Council.

In his *Juris Publici Ecclesiastici Institutiones* published in Rome, he speaks as follows:—" In temporal matters, and with respect to a temporal scope, the Church has no authority over the State. This is proved by reason: For whatsoever is done in temporal matters, having in view a temporal end, is outside the object of the Church. Now it is a general rule, that no society hath power beyond its own scope. And again, it is proved from the teaching of the Church. For Pope Gelasius writes to the Emperor Anastasius: 'As far as concerns the order of civil government, the Bishops of the Church obey thy laws, knowing that thou hast from God thine imperial order.' And St. Gregory the Great writes to Leo the Isaurian: 'As the Pontiff has no right to interfere in the affairs of the imperial household, nor in conferring royal dignity, so neither hath the Emperor, &c.' Hence it follows that the State, although composed of Catholics, yet in temporal matters, and from a temporal point of view, is by no means

ubordinate to the Church, but quite independent of
her. And when all the Fathers speak of the indepen-
dence of the State from the Church, their sense is
plain." It will perhaps add to the significance and
value of this passage to note that its eminent author
was one of what Protestants call " an extreme school,"—
a son of S. Ignatius Loyola. The Church presents no
greater danger to the State now than she has done since
1829; our allegiance, and our relation and duties to the
State, have been in no way changed or diminished by
the Vatican Council.

But if it be urged that the Pope is made absolute
and independent, and that this is a grievous danger;
we reply that the Pope is bound by the moral and divine law, by the commandments of God, by the rules
of the gospel, and by every definition in faith and
morals that the Church has ever made. No man is
more bound by law than the Pope—a fact plainly
known to himself, and to every bishop and priest in
Christendom.* And one of the laws which bind him is
the law he has taught by the condemnation of the 63rd
proposition in the *Syllabus*, " It is lawful to refuse obedience to legitimate princes and even to rebel against
them." And has he not condemned every society that
plots against the Civil Power?

We might go further and answer those who taunt
us with questions as to our civil allegiance: (1.) by declaring that our allegiance to the Queen is more *entire*
than that of Protestants—and to illustrate our meaning, (we hope without disrespect), we might say with

---

* See further, Appendices A and B.

confidence, that if our Sovereign were to change he religion to-morrow, the allegiance of Catholics woul in no sense be impaired, whatever might be the atti tude of extreme Protestants and their appeals to th act of settlement. (2.) We might answer by declarin; that our civil allegiance is *firmer* than that of Protest ants, because it is based not merely on reason and con science, or the *private* interpretation of the Bible, bu also, and more firmly, on the teaching and authority of a Church which is, as we have shewn, by its institution Divine. In addition, therefore, to all grounds of alle giance professed by our non-Catholic countrymen, we add another, which is most sacred. Beyond these there are no guarantees for our loyalty and civil allegiance that we can either give or even imagine.

5. We commenced this letter with a statement of our general principles as to the obligations of civil and spiritual allegiance; we have shown the Divine consti tution and character of our Church, the binding and unchangeable nature of the Divine Law and of every definition made by the Church. And such, as we have exhibited by proofs and documents, is the nature and character of the Vatican Council, that it has added pos itively nothing to what existed before, beyond the legal definition of old truths.

But what is the theological purpose and drift of the " political " pamphlet which lies before us ? Is it seri ously to call in question the civil allegiance of English and Irish Catholics? Avowedly not. Mr. Gladstone is good enough to consider them to be better than their religion, to be loyal to their Queen in spite of its laws and tendency. You cannot, and you do not, accept this more than doubtful compliment. For the Catholic who should say that he was better than his religion, is not far from practical Apostasy. What then is the theological object of the pamphlet? It is a plot with which others are in collusion, and has a German type and origin—a plot not only to sow dissension among English Catholics, but to encourage disloyalty also towards the Vicar of Christ. " Tell us," the pamphleteer seems to say, " tell us without fear, tell us openly, tell us without declamation, and without ambiguity of words :—What would you do were the Vicar of Christ to attempt to levy war upon the Queen, to command her death, and to destroy this British Empire? Whom could you obey in a struggle between these two powers, each supreme in its order—between the Spiritual and the Temporal Sovereignties? Speak out like men, whilst we stand by and applaud you."

And you, dear children in Christ, you may reasonably ask this self-commissioned Inquisitor, by what right, by whose authority he approaches you with these insulting questions in his mouth? Has your civil allegiance been called into doubt in the Cabinet, or in the Legislature, or in the civil tribunals of the country? Then why submit to its being questioned by one who has not even the plea of being a minister of the Crown?

The object is not to strengthen your *civil* allegiance, which needs no tonics, but to weaken your *spiritual* fidelity, or if this cannot be, then your tender reverence, your love and honour for the great Spiritual Father of Christendom. 'But tell us, he still urges, What would you do, or at least what would you *think*, if Pius IX.

were to invade this island ; or to launch a thunderbolt against your Queen?'

A faithful Catholic and a loyal subject would resent this political catechizing as though it were publicly inquired of him—What would be his behaviour towards his mother were she to misconduct herself in public?—were she guilty of such and such acts? As we have every natural reason to love the honour of our mother, so have we every supernatural reason to shield the honour of the Vicar of our Lord, and to decline to entertain his enemies with a discussion on the remotest of possibilities, or the foolishest of follies.

But we have another and even a graver answer than this, drawn though this be out of the heart of man. The Apostle Paul shall reply. He shall reply to Mr. Gladstone in words of repeated warning. He has need of them to-day. " Avoid," he says, " foolish questions and contentions and strivings about the law, for they are unprofitable and vain " (*Tit.* iii. 9.) " Avoid foolish and old wives' fables, and exercise thyself unto godliness " (I. *Tim.* iv. 7). All these " profane and vain babblings " " minister questions rather than edification of God which is in faith. Now the end of the commandment is charity from a pure heart and a good conscience and an unfeigned faith, from which things some going astray, are turned aside unto vain babbling; desiring to be teachers of the law, understanding neither the things they say, nor whereof they affirm. But we know that the law is good if a man use it lawfully " (*I. Tim.* i. 4, 5, 6, 7, 8).

But if Mr. Gladstone shall insist with pertinacity, we will reply to him once more and ask him to point out the passage in which our Divine Lord cautions men against submission to the Spiritual Power? Did He caution them *against* submission because individuals in authority might make mistakes? Even of the Scribes and Pharisees, hateful as they were in His sight, He said "all things whatsoever they (seated on the chair of Moses) shall say to you, observe and do; but according to their works do ye not" (*Matt.* xxiii. 3.) Is, then, obedience to Spiritual authority a danger to be apprehended now?

And shall we at this hour of the day,—with our Spiritual Father and Teacher in prison, because he has "loved justice and hated iniquity," and remains among the Sovereigns of Europe the only great column of truth and justice, as well as of unfailing charity,—shall we contemplate him as running counter to the Law of God and to the definitions of the Church, in order to gratify Mr. Gladstone and others, whose *end* is neither edification nor our civil allegiance, but "foolish questions and contentions and strivings about the law?"

No, you will be faithful to your Queen and you will be faithful to your Pope. There can be no antagonism between the works of God, unless the sin of man create it.

6. The subject of the deposing power of the Pope has been brought forward again by Mr. Gladstone and others; not, however, as though it formed a practical danger to any existing State, however wicked. The question whether this power comes within the authority bestowed upon St. Peter and his successors is purely speculative. It is no matter of Catholic faith, and is properly relegated to the schools. But this we must

say, to fear the result of this purely speculative question is scarcely consistent with the common sense of a practical people, like the English. It would form as useful and seasonable a subject of discussion at the present day as it would have been at Jerusalem or Rome, had the *quid nuncs* of those days sat down to examine whether Peter, when "sleeping between two soldiers, and bound with two chains" (Acts xii.), could have deposed King Herod ; or whether, when he lay in the nethermost prison of the Mamertine he could have dethroned the infamous Nero. To these passing observations we will add,—

(1). That there is no mention of this power in the *Syllabus* or in the *Enchiridion Symbolorum et Definitionum Fidei*.

(2). That no one has ever breathed the idea of Pius IX. exercising it, even in the case of King Victor Emmanuel.

(3). That when, in the centuries of undivided Christendom, it was used at the request of the oppressed against their wicked and unjust oppressors ; it was used very seldom ; with great formality; after fruitless admonitions and invitations to amend ; as an act of justice ; and finally its execution was left entirely to the people.

When Mr. Gladstone, as Prime Minister of the Crown, introduced a Court of Arbitration to settle international differences, he unconsciously justified this principle, that in the proper constitution of human society there is a need of a Supreme Judge in the cause of justice " by which kings reign."

(4). During this century over thirty Sovereigns have

been violently deposed by factions of their subject populations. Is it a question whether Sovereigns have gained by the exchange of the Supreme Tribunal of the Pope for the supreme tribunal of the mob? or whether civil allegiance is more sacred and inviolable now than when united Christendom carried the Vicar of Christ in triumph as the Supreme Arbiter and Judge of Israel?*

(5). Lastly, we would respectfully observe that those who are so sensitively tender at the mention of the indirect deposing power of the Pope (though it will never, as we believe, be exercised again), on the ground that religion has no right to trench on the civil authority, would do well to remember, that were the Sovereign of this Empire—including from 9,000,000 to 10,000,000 of Catholics—to change her religion for that of the Catholic Church, she would thereby, *ipso facto*, cease to reign, and be deposed. So that it would appear that the principle of the authority of religion, even in civil matters, is admitted in the British Constitution, which lays down that an English sovereign who does not profess the Protestant religion is unable or unfit to reign.

7. Does any one object that in consequence of the Vatican Council, or of their Religious Creed, Catholic electors or members of Parliament are not free to vote as they please, or that their political freedom is curtailed by their Church?

Mr. Gladstone has not raised this question in terms, but he has covertly implied it. You, brethren, can give the answer, You are as free as others to follow

* See Appendix C.

your reason and conscience in the discernment of the moral character of the various political questions which come before you. To say that your conscience and reason are illumined by the general principles of Catholic Faith and morality, is simply to say that you are Catholics. But in their particular application in common political life you are each one of you as free to judge and act as any Protestant. You know, from your own experience, how free you are in all matters of simple politics. When we ourselves think it right to lay before you our view of a political measure, you are neither bound nor expected to adopt our view if your conscience and reason think us mistaken. But is not the Pope brought in on every occasion? This is part of the "great Protestant Tradition" of Exeter Hall, which believes the Pope to be a *Deus ex machinâ*, and a good Catholic, a knave, or a fool.*

But at least it will be admitted that the Catholic vote helped to throw out the Gladstone Government.

We fully admit the allegation. It is perfectly true that the Irish Catholic members and many Catholic electors in England indirectly, contributed to the defeat of a Government with which, on most points, they had been in sympathy. They acted, each one freely and upon his own choice, in the application of a Catholic general principle, viz., that Education *must be* Religious. Mr. Gladstone resents their choice in differing from himself,—*hinc illæ lacrymæ*.

8. The Catholic Church is charged with statements made by English and Irish Prelates prior to the pass-

* See Appendix D.

ing of the Catholic Emancipation Bill; statements which could not, indeed, be made now in all respects, but which Mr. Gladstone tells us " powerfully operated on the open and trustful temper of this [English] people to induce them to grant . . . the great and just concession of 1829." We are perfectly ready to undertake the defence of these Prelates, and that upon the most solid grounds; but it need not be now.

If, however, they be accused of minimising doctrine, what shall we say of the reservation, the minimising of history, practised "on the open and trustful temper of the English people," by Mr. Gladstone, in his "Political Expostulation?" He has been pleased to ignore the real motives upon which the Catholic Emancipation Bill was passed, in order to attach a stigma upon the good faith of the Catholic Church towards the English people. These real motives must have been present to the mind of a Statesman living in the very light of the history of his own time; but they will not be present to the mind of, they will never have been even heard of by, millions among whom this political, "No Popery" pamphlet is being industriously circulated at reduced price.

In order, therefore, that the facts which led to your Emancipation may be present at least to your mind, we venture to lay before you the following extracts from well known historical authorities :—

In the *Memoirs by Sir Robert Peel*, (London, John Murray, 1856), Part I., pp. 365, 366, we read :—

"I do solemnly affirm, . . . that in advising and promoting the measures of 1829, I was swayed by no fear except the fear of public calamity, and that I acted throughout on a deep conviction that those measures were not only conducive to the general welfare, but that they had become imperatively necessary in order to avert from interests which had a special claim upon my support—the interests of the Church and of institutions connected with the Church—an imminent and increasing danger."

See also, pp. 360–362, Peel's letter to the Bishop of Limerick, in which he enumerates six reasons for the concession, without a word implying that he was influenced by any statements of Catholics repudiating Papal dictation.

To the same purpose is his memoranda on the question, pp. 284–294, and pp. 300–308.

In *The Greville Memoirs* (Longmans, 1874), Vol. I., pr 133, Chapter 4 [1828], occur the following:—

"The success of the Catholic question depends neither on Whigs nor Tories; the former of whom have not the power, and the latter not the inclination to carry it. The march of time and the state of Ireland will effect it in spite of everything, and its slow but continued advance can neither be retarded by its enemies nor accelerated by its friends."

P. 168, "It was the Clare election which convinced both him (Peel) and the Duke that it must be done. . . . If the Irish Catholics had not brought matters to this pass by agitation and association, things might have remained as they were for ever, and all these Tories would have voted on till the day of their death against them." Read the whole of Ch. V., pp. 164–220. See also *Guizot's Memoirs of Sir Robert Peel* (Bentley, 1857).

P. 40, in Sir R. Peel's opening speech, he says:—
"I yield, therefore, to a moral necessity which I cannot control, unwilling to push resistance to a point which might endanger the establishments that I wish to defend."

Again, read in the *Life of the Duke of Wellington*, by J. H. Stocqueler, vol. II., (1853,) the speech of Wellington, April, 1829:—
"I call on those who apprehend that danger (viz., to the Established Church) to state clearly whether that danger, on this particular occasion, is more to be expected as resulting from legislation or *from violence.*"

Again, in the *Life and Character of Sir Robert Peel*, by Sir Lawrence Peel, 1860, we have this testimony:—
"Their conduct has been stigmatised as a concession to violence. . . . Concession of this nature to the demands of an excited people, whether of a whole empire or of a part, will be judged from the nature of the demand and the motives of those who yield to it."

And lastly, we might refer to the *Life of the Duke of Wellington*. By Sir James Edward Alexander, 1840, Vol. II., Ch. x., pp. 439-471.

In his speech, April 2, 1829, Wellington referred to the prospect of civil war as his chief motive for having brought in the Bill, p. 463:
"If I could avoid, by any sacrifice whatever, even one month of civil war in the country to which I am attached, I would sacrifice my life in order to do it." See again details, in his speech in reply, p. 468.

9. It is manifestly impossible to treat at length of many details within the compass of a Pastoral letter.

But whilst Mr. Gladstone is flooding* the country with copies of his indictment against your honor and your religion, we must indicate, as it were with the tip of the pen, the character of one more point which is of some importance.

(1.) Mr. Gladstone is as unskilled and unlearned in the scientific and technical language used by the Pastors of the Catholic Church among themselves as he is prejudiced against the Faith itself. Law and Medicine have their own precise terminology and language, and the uninitiated cannot read them. It is so, precisely, with Catholic theology viewed as a science. The Encyclicals and the Syllabus were addressed not to the people, but to the Episcopate, by the Vicar of Christ. Those who have been accustomed to consider Bishops as civil functionaries, religion as an appanage of the State, and to determine doctrine by lay tribunals, may perhaps be pardoned if they forget that, in dealing with the Catholic Church, they have to do with a wholly different order of ideas, and are out of their depth until they have sat under scientific teachers, as Paul at the feet of Gamaliel. It is for the Bishops to expound the true sense of the scientific language of the Catholic Church.†

(2.) While far from saying that the doctrines of the Syllabus are acceptable to the world, or that the world will ever relish them in their entirety until it has been reconverted to the Gospel of Truth, we unhesitatingly

---

* It is publicly stated that 73,000 copies have been issued up to the present time.

† See the remarkable Pastoral of the Bishop of Birmingham. *Burns and Oates.*

affirm that Mr. Gladstone has so distorted the meaning of the propositions of the Syllabus as to make it a mockery of the Church's doctrine. We are prepared to show that the propositions which have been most misrepresented and misunderstood are to be found *in principle*, like hard-set mortar, in the deep foundations of the Constitution of England.

IX.—CONCLUSION.

From all that has been said we draw these three conclusions :—

1. No human being, or human organization, stands between us and our Civil Sovereign. Conscience, and reason, and the law of God, alone can come between us. A divine, and not a human teacher, interprets for us the law of God. We are not the subjects of a Foreign Power. The Pope, as Vicar of Christ, is to us no more a foreigner than Jesus Christ. Our civil allegiance is undivided and without limit in its own order.

2. They do not " forfeit mental and moral freedom " who are taught by a Divine Teacher. But they are *not* mentally and morally free who, having heard of such a Teacher, do not seek Him, or who having found Him, reject His teaching.

3. Mr. Gladstone " has conjured " up a phantom which it will be well for him if he can " conjure down." On a mistaken plea, and starting on an assumed premise, he endeavours to kindle political and civil hate among the united people of a Great Empire. We do not wish to suppose that he has

done this evil for power or place; he cannot have done it in the calm of an Imperial Statesman. The judgment of motives we leave to others.

Finally, we feel, dear brethren, no alarm. The discussion of our doctrines, even through contradiction, will further Truth. The English people are not to be duped within a quarter of a century by two Durham Letters. The chief organs of the Press within this Diocese, the men of business in our populous towns, the strength and manhood of a common-sense people, have appreciated the situation. In religion, we are, alas, divided; but in civil life and mutual confidence we are as *one*. For ourselves and flock we are satisfied to leave the verdict on our allegiance, and on our political and civil conduct to the fair judgment of the English people.

We "*commend you to God and to the word of His Grace.*" (Acts xx. 32.)

"*May the God of hope fill you with all peace and joy in believing; that you may abound in hope and in the power of the Holy Ghost.*" (Rom. xv. 13.)

"*Walk circumspectly . . . for the days are evil.*" (Eph. v. 15, 16.)

Given at Salford, on the Feast of S. Francis Xavier, December 3rd, 1874, and commanded to be read, in part, in all our Chapels and Churches, and to be circulated, in its entirety, among the members of our Flock.

✠ HERBERT, *Bishop of Salford.*

C. J GADD, *Secretary.*

APPENDICES.

APPENDIX A.

Dr. von Döllinger on the growth, office, power, limitations and perpetuity of the Papacy.

Let us hear the matured historical testimony of one whom Mr. Gladstone describes as "the most famous and learned living theologian of the Roman Communion, Dr. von Döllinger,"—although he had already assigned to Dr. Newman the place of "the first living theologian now within the Roman Communion." With Mr. Gladstone it seems that Ecclesiastical History and theology are the same, and that a Church Historian is always a theologian.

In regard to the following valuable extracts, we need only point out the strange absence of purely theological statements and arguments; this absence does not invalidate the Professor's testimony,—it will be accounted by some persons to strengthen it—but it leaves his narrative incomplete, and partially accounts for his recent defection.

In the following pages, then, taken from one of Dr. von Döllinger's last publications, "*The Church and the Churches*," (Hurst & Blackett, 1862,) may be seen what Mr. Gladstone calls "the truth and authority of history and the inestimable value of the historic spirit."

"Let us now approach somewhat nearer to the institution of the Papacy, which is comparable with no other; and let us cast a glance at its history. Like to all living things, like to the Church itself of which it is the crown and the corner-stone, the Papacy has passed through an historical development full of the most manifold and surprising vicissitudes. But in this its history is the law which lies at the foundation of the Church—the law of continual development—of a growth from within outwards. The Papacy had to pass through all the changes and circumstances of the Church, and to enter with it into every process of construction. Its birth begins with two mighty, significant, and far-extending words of the Lord. He to whom these words were addressed, realised them in his own person and actions, and planted the institution of the infant Church in the central point—at Rome. There it silently grew, *occulto velut arbor aevo ;* and in the oldest time it only showed itself forth on peculiar occasions; but the outlines of the power and the ecclesiastical authority of the Roman Bishops were ever constantly becoming more evident and more prominent. The Popes were, even in the time of the Roman Emperors, the guardians of the whole Church, exhorting and warning in all directions, disposing and judging, ' binding and loosing.' Complaints were not seldom expressed of the use which, in particular cases, Rome had made of its power. Resistance was offered, because the Pope was supposed to have been deceived; an appeal was preferred to him, when it was believed he had been better informed; but there was no refusal to obey his commands. In general, his interference in Church affairs was less necessary; and the reins of Church discipline needed less to be drawn tightly, so long as the general Church, with few exceptions, was found within the limits of the Roman Empire, when it was so firmly kept together by the strong bands of the civil order, that there could neither be occasion nor prospect of success to any reaction on the part of various nationalities, which, on the whole, were broken and kept down by Roman domination." (p. 41.)

"What is now, and in point of fact, the actual function and vocation of the Papacy, and why is the whole existence of the Church at this time, and in future, so inseparably bound up with the existence of the papal authority, and with its free exercise?"

"The Catholic Church is a most opulent, and, at the same time, a most multifarious organism. Its mission is nothing less than to be the teacher and moulder of all nations; and however much it may find itself hampered in this task; however limited may be the sphere of action allowed to it, by this or that government, its task always remains the same, and the Church requires and possesses an abundance of power to attain its purpose; it has a great number of various institutions, all directed to the same end, and with these it is continually creating new. All these powers, these institutions, these spiritual communities, stand in need of a supreme guidance, with a firm and strong hand, in order that they may work harmoniously together; that they may not degenerate, and may not lose sight of their destination; that they may not suicidally turn their capabilities, one against the other, or against the unity and welfare of the Church. It is only an ecclesiastical primacy can fulfil this mission—it is the Papacy alone that is in a position to keep every member in its own sphere, and to pacify every disturbance that may arise."

"Besides this, there is another task, just as difficult as it is important, which it lies upon the Papal See to fulfil."

"It is the duty, namely, of the Pope to represent and to defend the rights of individual Churches against the domination of states and monarchs; to watch that the Church be not altered in its character, nor crippled in its power, by becoming interwoven with the State. For this purpose, with the voice and action of the church immediately concerned, the intervention of the Supreme Church authority becomes indispensable; since this stands above and outside of the conflicts, which may possibly arise between any one church and the state; and it solely is capable in its high and inaccessible position, and in possession of the richest experiences, won in centuries of ecclesiastical government, to specify accurately the claims of both parties, and so serve as a stay and support to the weaker—to the one which otherwise must inevitably succumb before the manifold means of compulsion and seduction which lie at the command of modern states."

"It is, moreover, a beautiful, sublime, but certainly difficult mission of the Papal See—a mission only to be fulfilled by the strength of an enlightened wisdom and a comprehensive knowledge of mankind—and that is, to be just to the claims of individual nations in the Church; to comprehend their necessities, and restrain their desires within the limits required by the unity of the Church."

"For all this there is wanted a power opulently endowed with manifold views and prerogatives. If there were a primacy of dignity and honour, without any real power, the Church would be but badly served. This is not the place to enumerate all the particular rights which the Pope exercises in the ordinary course of his administration over the Church. They may be found in every hand-book of ecclesiastical law. But concerning the measure and extent, the limitation or illimitability of the Papal power, a few words, amid the prevailing confusion of ideas on the subject, cannot be considered as superfluous."

"Outside of the Catholic Church it has become almost a common form of speech—to brand the Papal power as being boundless, as being absolutist, as one which recognizes no law capable of controlling it. There is a great deal of talk of 'Romish omnipotence,' or of one at least with a never unceasing pretension to universal dominion. Persons maintain that 'Rome never foregoes a claim which she has once put forward; that she keeps such constantly in view, and upon every favourable opportunity strives to enforce it. All these representations and accusations are untrue and unjust. The Papal power is in one respect the most restricted that can be imagined, for its determinate purpose is manifest to all persons; and as the Popes themselves have innumerable times openly declared that purpose, 'to maintain the laws and ordinances of the Church, and to prevent any infringement of them.' The Church has long since had its established ordinances and its legislation determined on, even to the most minute points. The Papal See is thus, then, before all others, called upon to give an example of the most rigid adherence to Church tenets; and it is only upon this condition that it can rely upon obedience to itself on the part of individual churches, or calculate upon the respect of the faithful. Hence every one thoroughly well grounded in a knowledge of ecclesiastical legislation can, in most cases, with certainty anticipate what the Papal decision will be. Besides this, a considerable portion of Church ordinances rests, according to the views of Catholics, on the Divine Commandment, and are consequently for every one, and of course for the Papal power also, not to be tampered with. The Pope cannot dispense with things which are commanded by Divine Law. This is universally acknowledged. What, then, can restrain the Pope? De Maistre says, ' Everything—canons, laws, national customs, monarchs, tribunals, national assemblies, prescription, remonstrances, negotiations, duty, fear, prudence, and especially public opinion, the Queen of the World.' "

"In another respect, the Papal authority is certainly truly sovereign and free, one, too, which, according to its nature and purpose for extraordinary accidents and exigencies, must be endowed with an altogether extraordinary power to control every mere human right, and to permit or ordain exceptions to general rules. It may occur that serious embarrassments, new situations of things, may be placed before the Church; and to which existing ecclesiastical ordinances do not extend, and in which a solution can be found only by overstepping the regulations in force. If the necessity of the case requires it, 'the Pope,' as Bossuet says, 'can do l,'* of course with the exception of what is contrary to the Divine Law." (pp. 44-7.)

"The delusion that the Papal See has arrogated to itself a despotic and absolute power, and exercised it wherever it was not restrained by fear, is so generally diffused, especially in Germany and England—it is so customary to proclaim the boundlessness of that power, and the defencelessness in which individual Churches and persons find themselves when opposed to it, that I cannot refrain from exposing the error by a few decisive testimonies. Let us hear on this matter one who was a pope himself—Pius VII.:—

"'The Pope,' he says, in an official document drawn up in his name, and having reference to Germany †— The Pope is bound by the nature and the institutions of the Catholic Church, whose head he is, within certain limits, which he dare not overstep, without violating his conscience, and abusing that supreme power which Jesus Christ has confided to him to employ for the building up, and not the destruction, of His Church. Inviolable limits for the head of the Church are the dogmas of the Catholic faith, which the Roman bishops may, neither directly nor indirectly, violate; and although in the Catholic Church faith has always been regarded as unalterable, but discipline as alterable, yet the Roman bishops have, with respect even to discipline, in their actual conduct, always held certain limits sacred, although by this means they acknowledge the

---

* "Defens. Declar.," 2, 20; Oeuvres," vol. xxxiii. p. 354.

† "Esposizione dei sentimenti de Sua Santita," in the treatise, "Die Neuesten Grundlagen der Deutsch-Katholischen Kirchenverfassung." Stuttgart, 1821, p. 334.

obligation never to undertake any novelty in certa‍[in] things, and also not to subject other parts of disciplin‍[e] to alterations, unless upon the most important and irr‍[e]pugnable grounds. With respect to such principle‍[s] the Roman bishops have never thought that they cou‍[ld] admit any change in those parts of discipline which a‍[re] directly ordained of Jesus Christ Himself; or of tho‍[se] which, by their nature, enter into a connection wi‍[th] dogmas; or of those which may have been attacked b‍[y] erroneous believers to sustain these innovations; or als‍[o] in those parts on which the Roman bishops, on accou‍[nt] of the consequences that might result to the disparag‍[e]ment of religion and of Catholic principles, do not thin‍[k] themselves entitled to admit a change, whatever th‍[e] advantages might be offered, or whatever the amou‍[nt] of evils might be threatened.

"'So far as concerns other parts of Church disc‍[i]pline, which are not comprehended in the classes abov‍[e] mentioned, the Roman Bishops have felt no hesitatio‍[n] in making many changes; but they have always bee‍[n] grounded on the principles on which every well-ordere‍[d] society rests; and they have only given their conser‍[t] to such changes when the need or the welfare of th‍[e] Church required them.'" (pp. 47–9.)

"Cardinal Antonelli, Prefect of the Propagand‍[a] (under whom the Irish Bishops are placed), addresse‍[d] on the 23rd June, 1791, a Rescript to the Archbishop‍[s] and Bishops of Ireland, wherein it was said:—'W‍[e] must very carefully distinguish between the real right‍[s] of the Apostolic See, and what have been, with an in‍[i]mical intention, in modern times imputed to it. Th‍[e] Roman See has never taught that faith was not to b‍[e]

ept with 'heretics;' or, 'that an oath of allegiance made to kings, in a state of separation from a Catholic community, could be broken;' or, '*that it was allowable for a Pope to interfere with their temporal rights and possessions.*' This Rescript has been often enough printed, and I do not know what could be said more clearly or distinctly." * (p. 50.)

"Who will pronounce on the immediate future? Do we know what is coming in Germany? Are we in Central Europe not approaching some mighty convulsion? Is not the Mazzini party lurking behind Piedmont to hurl Italy into the throes and tortures of a social and anti-christian revolution? Who can say how much in Italy and elsewhere will meet destruction? One thing, however, is certain. Amidst all wrecks, one institution will remain erect, will constantly emerge from the flood of revolution—for it is indestructible, immortal—it is the Chair of St. Peter. If I am asked whence I draw this assurance, I may point to the Bible as my answer—'Thou art the Rock,' &c. But I will give another answer, derived from the very nature of the thing itself: The Papal See will not be destroyed, because it is reachable by no human power; because no one on earth is strong and powerful enough to destroy it. If all the Powers of Europe were to unite for its destruction, they could not effect it. All that human power can do is to compel it to make a pilgrimage; and, for a longer or shorter time, to keep its seat away from Rome. And, lastly, this Chair will not be

---

* See "Ami de la Religion," vol. xviii.; also in the works of Archbishop Affre of Paris, "Essai sur la Suprematie temp. du Pape,"

destroyed, because it is indispensable and irreplaceabl[e]
for it forms the keystone of the whole building of t[he]
Church. '*On ne détruit que ce qu'on remplace.*' Th[at]
the Papacy can ever be replaced by anything else, [no]
one will seriously maintain. It is the keystone th[at]
holds the whole edifice of the Church together, th[at]
makes the Church what it is and what it ought to b[e]
a world-Church—the only society that has in earne[st]
fulfilled the given purpose of God—that is, to embra[ce]
all humanity, and find room for all nations."

"Should this all-keeping, all-sustaining keysto[ne]
be taken away, the whole will fall asunder, the Chur[ch]
will be split according monarchies and nationalitie[s]
from the Christian religion will be rent that noble jew[el]
bestowed by her founders; that privilege that stan[ds]
alone in history—the privilege and the strength [to]
unite all nations in one great whole, yet without inju[ry]
to them as nations. The faithful throughout the wo[rld]
desire not to belong to a French or a Spanish, a B[a]-
varian or an Austrian Church; they desire to belo[ng]
to ONE church, THE Church, the only Catholic Chur[ch]
—in other words, all will be subject to the Pope, a[nd]
will, in community with him, feel and acknowled[ge]
themselves as members of 'the Catholic Church.'"

"The Papacy, then, will continue, because G[od]
wills it, because every Catholic believes it, becau[se]
two hundred millions of men in all parts of the wo[rld]
desire it, because everyone who knows the conditi[on]
of the world acknowledges it. There are enemies[,]
many enemies—of the Temporal Power of the Papac[y,]
but, within the Catholic world, there lives no enem[y]
of the Pope's Spiritual Power, or only such as are

1e same time the enemies of the Christian religion."
). 470.)

APPENDIX B.
Innocent III.'s limitation of the Papal Power.

It is difficult to make a selection from the vast umber of Papal documents which indicate the scope, nd at the same time the limitation of the Roman 'ontiff's power. We quote the following, written in 204, when the Papacy was in the zenith of its prestige nd influence, from the famous letter, *Novit Ille*, of nnocent III. to the Bishops of France, in the matter f the dispute between Philip and John, the Kings of 'rance and England.

"No person should imagine that we pretend to isturb or diminish the jurisdiction of the illustrious <ing of the French, any more than he desires to inter- ere with ours. . . . We do not pretend to pro- ounce judgment as to the fief, judgment on this natter belongs to his jurisdiction; but we pronounce *s to the sin.* To censure sin belongs, without doubt, o our office, and we can, and we ought, to exercise his office irrespectively of persons. The Royal dignity hould not consider itself slighted by submitting on his subject to the Apostolic judgment, for the Em-)eror Valentinian said to the Suffragans of Milan, 'Set ip for us a Bishop before whom, we ourselves who ;overn the Empire, may sincerely bow our head, and rom whom we, as men subject to sin, may receive leedful advice, as medicine from a physician.' . . .

Seeing that we do not rest our authority upon a human constitution, but rather upon a Constitution which i Divine,—our authority being not of man, but of God —every one knows that it is part of our office t(administer correction for all grievous sin to every Christian, and to visit with Ecclesiastical censure those who despise correction."—*Hist. de l'Eglise*, by Rohrbacher, vol. 17, p. 285.

APPENDIX C.

Curious statistical contrast arising out of " the rights of man," and the deposing Power of the Popes.

Mgr. Gaume, in his work on *La Situation*, in 1860 gave some curious statistics, which being corrected down to 1875, now stand as follows:—Since the famous "Rights of man" were proclaimed at the end of last century 45 thrones have been overthrown, 25 royal families driven into exile, 34 Charters or Constitutions drawn up, sworn to, and destroyed. As a vindication of the "Rights of man," within the span of one human life this is grimly significant. The legal depositions pronounced by Pontiffs through all the centuries scarcely reach a dozen. But then the Pontiffs have always taught the "Duties of man," and that through their performance are secured his rights.

APPENDIX D.

On the interference of the Clergy in certain political questions.

There can be no doubt but that the Sovereign

Pontiff, as Supreme Judge of the moral and divine law, has a right to pass a judgment upon the moral character of civil Constitutions, when he considers that the good of Religion, of human Society, and the law of God demand this of him. Thus, Pius IX. pronounced judgment in 1852 upon the religious portion of the iniquitous Constitution passed by the Government of New Granada, and in 1856 upon a part of that proclaimed by the Juarez Government of Mexico. In like manner he indirectly condemned the godless Colleges in Ireland, by declaring them to be unfit schools for the education of Catholic youth.

A remark will not be out of place here upon a peculiar view which has sometimes been put forward, viz.: that Ecclesiastics have no right to take any part in politics, and that they practically forfeit their civil rights by becoming Priests. There is in this theory one element of truth, and two elements of error. The element of truth is this obvious fact, that it is unfitting that one who has been consecrated to the service of God by the unction of the Priesthood, and has devoted his life to the direct cure of souls, should spend his time and his energies in the purely political arena. Such a course of conduct in one thus placed would lead to neglect of duty, and might involve positive injustice towards the souls of whose care he had accepted the responsibility. But the first element of error comes in when it is asserted that a man by becoming a Priest thereby forfeits the civil and political liberty enjoyed by his fellow countrymen, to think, speak, and write in behalf of civil and political justice. This is to introduce something worse than the system of castes. It is the mystical abstraction from human things practised by Brahmins. That it is highly desirable that the Clergy should mix as little as possible in simple politics and party warfare, that they should live in a sphere removed from mere earthly and temporal contentions, and thus render their sacred ministry more acceptable and more effective is undeniable. But a second element of error, more mischievous than the first, urges sometimes in the name of religion itself, that, though a political question trench upon the truths of Religion, though the interests of the Divine law and the salvation of souls be directly concerned in a political measure, a clergyman's duty is to remain a silent, passive, and perhaps indifferent spectator, simply because he is a clergyman :—that his voice must be silent in the pulpit and on the platform if the subject in contention have a political as well as a direct religious bearing. This was in reality the theory of the revolutionist, Terenzio Mamiani, when he insolently advised Pius IX. "to inhabit peaceably the serene sphere of dogma," and abandoning all the practical concerns of men, to be satisfied " to pray, to bless, and to pardon." It is the consistent theory of those who seek, or applaud, the destruction of the temporal power.

Putting aside, then, these errors, we may affirm that just as the Sovereign Pontiff speaks, when occasion requires, with supreme authority, upon the morality of political acts, so may it from time to time be the duty of Bishops to speak, and to direct the clergy subject to them to speak, in unambiguous terms on political measures which directly concern the cause of Divine Truth, Religion, and the salvation of souls. It is certain that a Spiritual Superior does not exceed the province of his authority, if he so far enters into political and temporal matters as to pass judgment upon their conformity with the moral and divine law. This is explicitly taught by S. Thomas. " Potestas saecularis subditur spirituali sicut corpus animae (ut Greg. Naz. dicit Orat. 17) et ideo non est usurpatum judicium, si spiritualis praelatus se intromittat de temporalibus *quantum ad ea in quibus* subditur ei saecularis potestas, vel quae ei a saeculari potestate relinquuntur." 2a 2ae q. 60. A 6. Ad 3m.

APPENDIX E.

On the Immaculate Conception, historically.

In the Note p. 3 of this Letter reference has been made to Mr. Gladstone's assertion that the definition of the Immaculate Conception was " a violent breach with history " and a " deadly blow at the old historic school."

Out of a thousand historical witnesses let us listen to the words of Peter of Celles, writing to Nicholas, Prior of St. Albans, in Hertfordshire, more than 700 years ago :—

" I believe, I say, I maintain, and I swear (these are his words,) that the Most Blessed Virgin was endowed with special privileges in her eternal predestination, nor from the moment of her conception did she suffer the slightest stain, but remained ever and preserved to the end in spotless integrity; and as she was blessed beyond human nature, so are her perfections sublime and hidden beyond human thought."—("*Our Lady's Dowry*," p. 31.)

While our English forefathers were beginning to establish the Festival of the Immaculate Conception without reference to the Holy See, this same Peter of Celles, Abbot of S. Rémi, and afterwards Bishop of Chartres, wrote to the English Prior as follows—and we make the quotation to show that the acts of 1854 and 1870 were not "a violent breach with history," but in perfect and harmonious sequence with the early History of the Church in England and France.

"I would far more willingly open the cataracts of Heaven and the fountains of the deep in honor of the Virgin than close them: nay, if her own Son Jesus—were such a thing possible—had left undone anything for the exaltation of His Mother, I, her servant and her slave, would try to make it up, if not in effect, at least in affection. I would rather have no tongue than use it against Our Lady. I would rather have no soul than diminish anything of the glory of hers. No doubt it was ever lawful and ever will be lawful for the Church, the Spouse of Christ, during her sojourn in the world, according to the changes of times and of persons and of things, to vary her decrees, and to find new remedies for new diseases, and to appoint new festivals for her saints. But gold and silver have a mint in which they must be coined—the Seat of Peter and the Court of Rome, which holds the principality and the keys of Heaven. It belongs to her to open to us, in the dispensation of God, the secrets of God's counsels, and the oil of grace runs down from the head (Aaron) to the borders of his vestment.

"This Seat of Peter, in which Moses sits—that is, in which resides 'the immaculate law which converts the soul'—this is the Rock which falls and crushes the gatherings of the heretics, which stops all profane novelties of word, which cuts off what is superfluous and fills up whatever is incomplete. I should then be glad indeed if this Mistress and Directress of Christendom, with the authority of truth, had weighed in the scales of a general consultation [this is precisely the course which was adopted by Pius IX. before the Definition of 1854] and had approved the festival of Our Lady's Conception, and had propagated it from sea to sea. If the sun, that is the Pope, and the moon, that is the Roman Church, had gone before, then no less quickly than securely would I have walked in their light, without fear of slipping or stumbling." ("*Our Lady's Dowry*," p. 27.)

THE CATHOLIC PUBLICATION SOCIETY'S BOOKS.

The Invitation Heeded. Reasons for a Return to Catholic Unity. By James Kent Stone, late President of Kenyon and Hobart Colleges. Fifth Edition, one vol. 12mo, ... $1 50

An Essay in Aid of a Grammar of Assent. By John Henry Newman, D.D., of the Oratory. One vol. 12mo, . . . $2 50

Catholic Tracts. Fifty Catholic Tracts of "The Catholic Publication Society," on various Subjects. One vol. 12mo, cloth extra, ... $1 25
The same, in paper covers,
single copies, . . . 60
25 copies, ... 9 00
50 copies, ... 17 00
100 copies, only. . . 30 00

Familiar Discourses to the Young. Preceded by an Address to Parents. By a Catholic Priest. One vol. 12mo, cloth, . $0 75
The same in paper, . . 30

Elia; or, Spain Fifty Years Ago. From the Spanish of Fernan Caballero. One vol. 12mo, $1 50

Impressions of Spain. By Lady Herbert. One vol. 12mo.

Fifteen Illustrations. Cloth, extra, ... $2 00
Cloth, gilt, ... 2 50
Half morocco or calf, . 3 50
Full calf, ... 6 00

The Life of St. Patrick, Apostle of Ireland. By M. F. Cusack, author of "The Illustrated History of Ireland," etc., etc. Illustrated. One vol. 4to, . . . $6 00

Glimpses of Pleasant Homes. By the Author of "The Life of Mother McCauley." Illustrated with four full-page illustrations. One vol. 12mo, cloth, extra, $1 50
Cloth, gilt, ... 2 00

Why Men do not Believe; Or, The Principal Causes of Infidelity. Translated from the French of Mgr. Laforet. Cloth, $1 00

Cradle Lands. Egypt, Syria, Palestine, Jerusalem, etc. By Lady Herbert. Illustrated by eight full-page illustrations. One vol. 12mo, vellum cloth, . . . $2 00
Cloth, full gilt, . . . 3 00
Half calf, ... 4 00
Full calf, extra, red edges, 6 00

An Illustrated History of Ireland, from the Earliest Period to

the Present Time; with several first-class full-page Engravings of Historical Scenes, designed by Henry Doyle, and engraved by George Hanlon and George Pearson: together with upwards of One Hundred Woodcuts, by eminent artists, illustrating Antiquities, Scenery, and Sites of Remarkable Events; and three large Maps, one of Ireland, and the others of Family Homes, Statistics, etc. One vol. 8vo, nearly 700 pages, extra cloth, $5 00
Half calf, ... 7 00

Irish Odes, and other Poems. By Aubrey de Vere. One vol. 12mo, toned paper, . . $2 00
Cloth, gilt, ... 2 50

The Works of the Most Reverend John Hughes, D.D., first Archbishop of New York, containing Biography, Sermons, Letters, Lectures, Speeches, etc. Carefully compiled from the Best Sources, and edited by Lawrence Kehoe. Two vols., cloth, bevelled, $8 00
Two vols., half calf, extra, large paper, . . . 12 00

The See of Peter, the Rock of the Church, the Source of Jurisdiction, and the Centre of Unity. By Thomas William Allies. One vol., cloth, ... $0 75

Anne Severin. By the Author of "A Sister's Story." One vol. 12mo, cloth, . . . $1 50
Cloth gilt, ... 2 00

In Heaven we Know Our Own. Translated from the French of Père Blot. One vol. 18mo, $0 60

Book of Irish Martyrs. Memorials of those who Suffered for the Catholic Faith in Ireland during the Sixteenth, Seventeenth, and Eighteenth Centuries. Collected and edited by Myles O'Reilly,
B.A., LL.D. One vol. crown 8vo, vellum cloth, . . . $2 50

Diary of a Sister of Mercy. Tales from the Diary of a Sister of Mercy. By C. M. Brame. One vol. 12mo. Extra cloth, . $1 50
Extra gilt, ... 2 00

Reason and Revelation. Lectures delivered in St. Anne's Church, New York, during Advent, 1867, by Rev. T. S. Preston. One vol. 12mo, . . . $1 50

Life and Letters of Madame Swetchine. Translated from the French of the Count Falloux. One vol. 12mo, ... $2 00

Catholic Hymns and Canticles. This edition contains twenty-one new Hymns; among which are five Christmas Carols, a charming carol for Easter, entitled "The Alleluia Bells;" several new and original Songs for Catechism; the popular Congregational Hymns sung in the Paulist Church by the Rosary and Christian Doctrine Societies, and at the Way of the Cross, etc., the whole forming the most complete Catholic Hymn Book ever published. One vol. 12mo, ... $1 00

The Office of Vespers. Containing the order of the Vesper Service; the Gregorian Psalm Tones, harmonized, with the Psalms for all the Vespers during the year pointed for chanting. By Rev. Alfred Young. With the Imprimatur of the Most Rev. Archbishop of New York. Single copies, . $0 75
Per dozen, ... 6 00

Three Phases of Christian Love. The Mother, the Maiden, and the Religious. By Lady Herbert. One vol. 12mo. . $1 50
Gilt, extra, ... 2 00

Aspirations of Nature. By Rev. I. T. Hecker. Fourth edition, revised, cloth extra. . . $1 50

Gropings After Truth. A Life-Journey from New England Congregationalism to the One Catholic Apostolic Church. By Joshua Huntington. One volume vellum cloth, ... $0 75

The Clergy and the Pulpit, in their Relations to the People. By M. l'Abbé Isidore Mullois, Chaplain to Napoleon III. One vol. 12mo, extra cloth, . . $1 50
Half calf, ... 2 00

Symbolism; or, Exposition of the Doctrinal Differences between Catholics and Protestants, as evidenced by their Symbolic Writings. By John A. Moehler, D.D. Translated from the German, with a Memoir of the Author, preceded by an Historical sketch of the State of Protestantism and Catholicism in Germany for the last Hundred Years, by J. B. Robertson, Esq., $4 00

The Comedy of Convocation in the English Church. In Two Scenes. Edited by Archdeacon Chasuble, D.D., and dedicated to the Pan-Anglican Synod. 8vo, cloth, ... $1 00

Life of Father Baker. The Life and Sermons of the Rev. Francis A. Baker, Priest of the Congregation of St. Paul. Edited by Rev. A. F. Hewit. One vol. crown 8vo, pp. 504, ... $2 50
Half calf or mor. extra, . 4 00

Sermons of the Paulist Fathers for 1864. New Edition. Cloth, extra, ... $1 50

Sermons of the Paulist Fathers, for 1865 and 1866. Cloth, extra, ... $1 50

Sermons of the Paulist Fathers. Sixth volume. Cloth, extra, ... $1 50

A Sister's Story. By Mrs. Augustus Craven. Translated from the French of Emily Bowles. One vol. crown 8vo, pp. 528. Cloth, extra, ... $2 50
Cloth, gilt, ... 3 00
Half calf, ... 4 00
Full calf, ... 7 00

St. Columba, Apostle of Caledonia. By the Count de Montalembert. One volume 12mo. Toned paper, ... $1 25
Cloth, gilt, ... 1 75

Problems of the Age. With Studies on St. Augustine on Kindred Subjects. By Rev. A. F. Hewit. One vol. 12mo. Extra cloth, ... $2 00

Christine, and other Poems. By George H. Miles. Cloth, $2 00
Gilt, extra, ... 2 50

The Illustrated Catholic Sunday-School Library. First Series of six vols., handsomely bound, and put up in a box. Cloth, ex., $3 00
Cloth, gilt, ... 4 00

The following are the titles of the six volumes comprising the First Series: Madeleine the Rosière; Crusade of the Children; Tales of the Affections; Adventures of Travel; Truth and Trust; Select Popular Tales.

The Illustrated Catholic Sunday-School Library. Second Series of six volumes, handsomely bound, and put up in a box. Cloth, extra, ... $3 00
Cloth, gilt, ... 4 00

The following are the titles of the six volumes comprising the Second Series: The Rivals; The Battle of Lepanto, etc.; Scenes and Incidents at Sea; The Schoolboys, and The Boy and the Man; Beautiful Little Rose; Florestine.

The Illustrated Catholic Sunday School Library. Third Series, six volumes, handsomely bound,

and put up in a box. Cloth, extra, ... $3 00
Cloth, gilt, ... 4 00

The following are the titles of the six volumes comprising the Third Series: Nettlethorpe, the Miser; Tales of Naval and Military Life; Harry O'Brien, and other Tales; The Hermit of Mount Atlas; Leo, or The Choice of a Friend; Antonio, or The Orphan of Florence.

The Illustrated Catholic Sunday-School Library. Fourth Series, six volumes, handsomely bound, and put up in a box. Cloth, extra, ... $3 00
Cloth, gilt, ... 4 00

The following are the titles of the six volumes comprising the Fourth Series: Tales of the South of France; Stories of other Lands; Emma's Cross, and other Tales; Uncle Edward's Stories; Joe Baker; The Two Painters.

The Illustrated Catholic Sunday-School Library. Fifth Series, six volumes, handsomely bound, and put up in a box. Cloth, extra, ... $3 00
Cloth, gilt, ... 4 00

The following are the titles of the six volumes comprising the Fifth Series: Bad Example; May Day, and other Tales; James Chapman; The Young Astronomer, and other Tales; Angel Dreams; Ellerton Priory.

The Illustrated Catholic Sunday-School Library. Sixth Series, six volumes, handsomely bound, and put up in a box. Cloth, extra, ... $3 00
Cloth, gilt, ... 4 00

The following are the titles of the six volumes comprising the Sixth Series: Idleness and Industry; The Hope of the Katzekopfs; St. Maurice; The Young Emigrants; Angels' Visits; Scrivener's Daughter, and Orange Girl.

The Illustrated Catholic Sunday-School Library. Seventh Series, six vols., handsomely bound, and put up in a box. Cloth, extra, ... $3 00
Cloth, gilt, ... 4 00

The following are the titles of the books in this Series: Tales of Catholic Artists; Honor O'More's Three Homes; Sir Ælfric, and other Tales; Select Tales for the Young; Tales for the Many; Frederick Wilmot.

Nellie Netterville; or, One of of the Transplanted. A Tale of the Times of Cromwell in Ireland. One vol. 12mo. Cloth, extra, . $1 50
Cloth, gilt, ... 2 00

The Holy Communion. Its Philosophy, Theology, and Practice. By John Bernard Dalgairns, Priest of the Oratory of St. Philip Neri. One vol. 12mo, . $2 00

Dr. Newman's Answer to Dr. Pusey's Eirenicon. Paper, $0 75

Questions of the Soul. By Rev. I. T. Hecker. New edition, ... $1 50
Cloth, gilt, ... 2 00

Apologia Pro Vita Sua. Being a Reply to a Pamphlet entitled "What, then, does Dr. Newman Mean?" By John Henry Newman, D.D. New edition. One volume, 12mo, ... $2 00

Exposition of the Doctrine of the Catholic Church in Matters of Controversy. By the Right Rev. J. B. Bossuet. A new edition, with copious notes, by Rev. J. Fletcher, D.D. 18mo, . . . $0 60
Another edition, without notes, 32mo, cloth, ... $0 25

Father Rowland. A North American Tale. 18mo, cl., $0 60

The Catholic Publication Society's Books. 5

An Amicable Discussion on the Church of England, and on the Reformation in general, dedicated to the clergy of every Protestant Communion, and reduced into the form of letters by the Right Rev. J. F. M. Trevern, D.D., Bishop of Strasbourg. Translated by the Rev. William Richmond. One volume 12mo, 580 pages, . . . $2 00

Anima Divota; or, Devout Soul. Translated from the Italian of Very Rev. J. B. Pagani, Provincial of the Order of Charity in England. 24mo, cloth, . . $0 60

Bona Mors: A Pious Association of the Devout Servants of our Lord Jesus Christ, dying on the Cross. In order to obtain a good death. 24mo, cloth, . . $0 25

Catholic Christian Instructed in the Sacraments, Sacrifices, Ceremonies, and Observances of the Church, by way of question and answer. By the Right Rev. Dr. Challoner. 24mo, cloth, flexible, $0 25

Catholic Christian Instructed. 12mo edition. Flexible cl., $0 50 Extra cloth, ... 75

Catechism of the Council of Trent. Published by Command of Pope Pius V. Translated by Rev. J. Donovan, Professor Royal College, Maynooth. 8vo, $2 00

The Life of Father Ravignan, S.J. By Father Ponlevoy, S.J. Translated from the French. One vol. crown 8vo, toned paper, $4 00

History of the Church from its Establishment to the Reformation. By the late Rev. C. C. Pise, D.D. Five vols. 8vo, . $7 50 Another edition, five vols. 12mo, cloth, ... $5 00

Historical Catechism. By M. l'Abbé Fleury. Parts I. and II.,
revised by Right Rev. Bishop Cheverus. 18mo, paper cover, $0 12 Complete in 4 parts. 18mo, 60

History of England, for the Use of Schools. By W. F. Myllus. Continued down to the present time, by John G. Shea, LL.D. 12mo, ... $1 25

Hornihold on the Commandments, Etc. The Commandments and Sacraments explained in Fifty-two Discourses. By the Right Rev. Dr. Hornihold, author of "Real Principles of Catholics." 12mo, cloth, ... $2 00

Home of the Lost Child. 18mo, cloth, ... $0 60

Letters of Eugenie de Guerin. Edited by G. S. Trebutien. One vol. 12mo, . . . $2 00

Journal of Eugenie de Guerin. Edited by G. S. Trebutien. One vol. 12mo, . . . $2 00

Abridgment of the Christian Doctrine. By the Right Rev. Bishop Hay. 32mo, cloth, $0 30

Compendious Abstract of the History of the Church of Christ. By Rev. William Gahan. With continuation down to the present time. By John G. Shea, LL.D. 12mo, ... $1 25

Confidence in the Mercy of God. Reflections on the Confidence in the Mercy of God. By the Right Rev. Joseph Languet. 18mo, cloth, ... $0 50

Defence of Catholic Principles. By the Rev. D. A. Gallitzin. Fourth edition. 18mo, cloth, $0 60

Genevieve. A Tale of Antiquity, showing the Wonderful Ways of Providence in the Protection of Innocence. From the German of Schmid. 18mo, cloth, **$0 60**

Grounds of the Catholic Doctrine, contained in the Profession of Faith published by Pope Pius IV.; to which are added, Reasons why a Catholic cannot conform to the Protestant Religion. 32mo, cloth, ... **$0 20**

History of the Old and New Testaments. By J. Reeve. 8vo, half-bound, embossed, roan, **$1 00**

Way of Salvation, its Meditations for Every Day in the Year. Translated from the Italian of St. Alphonsus Liguori. By Rev. James Jones. 24mo, cloth, . . **$0 75**

The Two Schools. A Moral Tale. By Mrs. Hughs. 12mo, cloth, ... **$1 00**

Sacred Heart of Jesus and the Sacred Heart of Mary. Translated from the Italian of Father Lanzi, author of "History of Painting," etc. With an introduction by Rev. C. P. Meehan. 24mo, cloth, ... **$0 60**

Short Treatise on Prayer. Adapted to all Classes of Christians. By St. Alphonsus Liguori. New edition, 24mo, cloth, . . **$0 40**

Spiritual Director of Devout and Religious Souls. By St. Francis de Sales, ... **$0 50**

Spirit of St. Alphonsus de Liguori. A Selection from his Shorter Spiritual Treatises. Translated from the Italian by the Rev. J. Jones. With a Memoir of the Author. 24mo, cloth, . **$0 60**

Spiritual Combat. To which is added, The Peace of the Soul and the Happiness of the Heart which dies to itself in order to live to God. 32mo, . . . **$0 40**

Poor Man's Controversy. By J. Mannock, author of "Poor Man's Catechism." 18mo, cloth, **$0 50**

Practical Discourses on the Perfections and Works of God, and the Divinity and Works of Jesus Christ. By Rev. J. Reeve. 8vo. cloth, ... **$2 50**

Visits to the Blessed Sacrament and to the Blessed Virgin, for Every Day in the Month. By St. Alphonsus Liguori. 24mo, cloth, new edition, . . . **$0 60**

Triumph of Religion; or, A Choice Selection of Edifying Narratives. Compiled from various authors, 18mo, cloth, . . **$0 60**

Stories on the Seven Virtues. By Agnes M. Stewart, Authoress of *Festival of the Rosary*. 18mo, cloth, ... **$0 60**

Nouet's Meditations on the Life and Passion of Our Lord Jesus Christ, for Every Day in the Year. By Rev. J. Nouet, S.J. To which are added, Meditations on the Sacred Heart of Jesus Christ, being those taken from a Novena in preparation for the Feast of the same. By Father C. Borgo, S.J. One vol. 12mo, 880 pages, . . . **$2 50**

Spiritual Consoler; or, Instructions to Enlighten Pious Souls in their Doubts and Allay their Fears. Written originally in Latin by Father Quadrupani. 18mo. **$0 50**

Net for the Fishers of Men. **$0 06**

Oratory of the Faithful Soul; or, Devotions to the most Holy Sacrament and to Our Blessed Lady. Translated from the works of Venerable Abbot Blosius. By Robert Aston Coffin, Priest of the Oratory. 18mo, cloth, . **$0 50**

The Catholic Publication Society's Books. 7

Life of St. Vincent de Paul.
32mo, cloth, ... $0 45

May Carols, and Hymns and Poems. By Aubrey de Vere. Blue and gold, ... $1 25

Little Treatise on the Little Virtues. Written originally in Italian by Father Roberti, of the Society of Jesus. To which are added, A Letter on Fervor by Father Vallois, S.J., and Maxims from an unpublished manuscript of Father Signeri, S.J.; also, Devotions to the Sacred Heart of Jesus. 32mo, cloth, ... $0 45

Love of Our Lord Jesus Christ reduced to Practice. By St. Alphonsus Liguori. Translated by the Right Rev. W. Walsh, Bishop of Halifax. New edition, 18mo, cloth, ... $0 60

Hours of the Passion; or, Pathetic Reflections on the Sufferings and Death of our Blessed Redeemer. By St. Liguori. New edition. Translated by Right Rev. W. Walsh, Bishop of Halifax, with a sketch of the Life of St. Alphonsus Liguori. 18mo, cloth, $0 60

Memorial of a Christian Life. Containing all that a soul newly converted to God ought to do that it may attain the perfection to which it ought to aspire. By Rev. Lewis de Granada, O.S.D. Revised and corrected by Rev. F.J. L'Estrange, O.S.D. 18mo, cloth, . . $0 75

Month of Mary; Containing a Series of Meditations, etc., in Honor of the B. V. M. Arranged for each day of the month. 32mo, cloth,
$0 40

Think Well On't; or, Reflections on the Great Truths of the Christian Religion, for every day in the month. By Right Rev. R. Challoner. 32mo, cloth, . $0 30

Office of the Holy Week, according to the Roman Missal and Breviary, in Latin and English. 18mo, cloth, ... $0 50
Roan, one plate, . . . 1 25
Roan, gilt edge, two plates, 1 75
Turkey mor., super extra, four plates, . . 3 50

Poor Man's Catechism; or, The Christian Doctrine Explained, with short admonitions. By John Mannock, O.S.B. 24mo, cloth,
$0 50

Lives of the Fathers of the Desert, and of many Holy Men and Women who dwelt in Solitude. Translated from the French. Embellished with eighteen engravings. 18mo, cloth, . . $0 60

Louisa; or, The Virtuous Villager. A Catholic Tale. New Edition. 18mo, cloth, . $0 60

Homilies on the Book of Tobias; or, A Familar Explanation of the Practical Duties of Domestic Life. By Rev. T. Martyn. 12mo, cloth, ... $1 00

Imitation of the Blessed Virgin, in Four Books. 18mo, cloth,
$0 60

Interior Christian, in Eight Books, with a Supplement. Extracted from the writings of M. Bernier de Louvigny. 18mo, cloth,
$0 60

Introduction to a Devout Life. From the French of St. Francis de Sales, Bishop and Prince of Geneva. To which is prefixed an abstract of his life. 18mo, cloth,
$0 75

Lenten Monitor; or, Moral Reflections and Devout Aspirations on the Gospel for each day, from Ash-Wednesday till Easter Sunday. By Rev. P. Baker, O.S.F. 24mo, cloth. New edition, . $0 60

Letter to a Protestant Friend on the Holy Scriptures. By Rev. D. A. Gallitzin. 18mo, cloth, $0 60

The Life of the Blessed Virgin S. Catharine of Sienna. One vol. 12mo, ... $1 75

An Epistle of Jesus Christ to the Faithful Soul that is devoutly affected toward Him; wherein are contained certain Divine Inspirations, teaching a man to know himself, and instructing him in the Perfection of True Piety. One vol. 16mo, ... $1 00

Letters to a Prebendary. Being an Answer to Reflections on Popery by Rev. J. Sturgis, LL.D. By Right Rev. J. Milner, D.D. 24mo, cloth, ... $0 75

The Office of Vespers. Containing the Order of the Vesper Service: the Gregorian Psalm Tones, harmonized, with the Psalms for all the Vespers during the year pointed for chanting. By Rev. Alfred Young. With the imprimatur of the Most Rev. Archbishop of New York. Single copies, $0 75

Hymns and Songs for Catholic Children, containing the most popular Catholic Hymns for every season of the Christian Year, together with May songs, Christmas and Easter carols for the use of Sunday-schools, sodalities, and confraternities. Paper covers, . $0 15
Cloth flexible, . . . 25

Life of Mother Margaret Mary Hallahan, Founder of the English Congregation of St. Catharine of Siena, of the Third Order of St. Dominic. By her Religious Children. With a Preface by the Right Rev. Bishop Ullathorne. 1 vol. 8vo, ... $4 00

Life of Mother Margaret Mary Hallahan. Abridged. One vol. 12mo, cloth extra, . . $1 50

Life, Passion, Death, and Resurrection of our Lord Jesus Christ. Being an Abridged Harmony of the Four Gospels in the Words of the Sacred Text. Edited by the Rev. Henry Formby. With over sixty engravings from original designs. One vol. 12mo, . $1 00

Early History of the Catholic Church in the Island of New York. By the Right Rev. J. R. Bayley, D.D. With four Steel plates of the four first Bishops and a Wood-cut of old St. Peter's. One vol. 12mo, $1 50

Christ and the Church. Lectures delivered in St. Ann's Church, New York, during Advent, 1869. By Rev. Thos. S. Preston. One vol. 12mo, ... $1 50

Life of Blessed Margaret Mary. With some account of the Devotion to the Sacred Heart. By the Rev. George Tickell, S.J. One vol. 8vo, ... $2 50

Illustrated Catholic Family Almanac for, 1869, 1870, 1871, 1872. 25 cents each.

Guide to Catholic Young Women. Especially for those who earn their own living. By Rev. George Dishon, Missionary Priest. One vol. 12mo, . . $1 00

Dion and the Sibyls: A Classic Christian Novel. By Miles Gerald Keon. One vol. 8vo, cloth extra, ... $1 50
The same in paper covers, 60

The Pictorial Bible and Church History. Stories Abridged and Complete. One vol. With a view of Solomon's Temple, a bird's-eye view of Jerusalem, and upwards of One Hundred beautiful

Engravings. Crown 8vo, 320 pp.
By Rev. Henry Formby. Cloth,
extra, ... $1 50
Cloth, gilt, ... 2 00
Half-calf, ... 3 50
Full-calf, ... 7 00

The Complete Sodality Manual and Hymn-Book. By the Rev. Alfred Young. One vol. 12mo, $1 00

The Life of Mother Julia, Foundress of the Sisters of Notre Dame. One vol. 12mo, cloth, extra. With portrait of Mother Julia, $1 50
Cloth, gilt, ... 2 00

Familiar Instructions on Mental Prayer. By the Abbé Courbon. Translated from the French, and edited by Rev. W. T. Gordon, of the Oratory, London, One vol. 16mo, cloth, . $0 75
Vellum cloth, limp, red edges, . . . 1 25

Light in Darkness: A Treatise on the Obscure Night of the Soul. By Rev. A. F. Hewit. One vol. 16mo, cloth extra, . $0 75
Cloth, limp, red edges, . 1 00

The House of Yorke. A Story of American Life. One vol. 8vo. Illustrated, . . $2 00
Cloth, gilt, ... 2 50

The Liquefaction of the Blood of St. Januarius. Paper, 50 cents; cloth, ... $1 00

Sermons on Ecclesiastical Subjects. By Archbishop Manning. American edition. Vol. I., $2 00
——— The same. Vol. II., 2 00

Maggie's Rosary, and other Tales, ... $1 00

Little Pierre, the Pedlar of Alsace. Translated from the French, and illustrated by 27 first-class woodcuts, . . . $1 50
Cloth, gilt, ... 2 00

Bibliographia Catholica Americana. By Rev. Joseph M. Finotti. To subscribers only, $3 00

Men and Women of the English Reformation. From the days of Wolsey to the death of Cranmer. Two vols, ... $4 00

Constance Sherwood. By Lady Fullerton. With illustrations. $2 00

The Betrothed. By Manzoni. One vol. 12mo, . . . $1 50

Manresa; or, The Spiritual Exercises of St. Ignatius, for General Use. One vol. 12mo, $1 50

THE CATHOLIC PUBLICATION SOCIETY,

LAWRENCE KEHOE, *General Agent,*

· No. 9 Warren Street, New York.

www.ingramcontent.com/pod-product-compliance
Lightning Source LLC
Chambersburg PA
CBHW020310090426
42735CB00009B/1291